POLITICS *in* AMERICA

Lecture Notes of a Lunatic Professor

DR. RANDY ARRINGTON

POLITICS IN AMERICA
Lecture Notes of a Lunatic Professor

iUniverse books may be ordered through booksellers or by contacting:

iUniverse
1663 Liberty Drive
Bloomington, IN 47403
www.iuniverse.com
1-800-Authors (1-800-288-4677)

Because of the dynamic nature of the Internet, any web addresses or links contained in this book may have changed since publication and may no longer be valid. The views expressed in this work are solely those of the author and do not necessarily reflect the views of the publisher, and the publisher hereby disclaims any responsibility for them.

Any people depicted in stock imagery provided by Thinkstock are models, and such images are being used for illustrative purposes only. Certain stock imagery © Thinkstock.

ISBN: 978-1-4917-8950-6 (sc)
ISBN: 978-1-4917-8952-0 (hc)
ISBN: 978-1-4917-8951-3 (e)

Library of Congress Control Number: 2016903020

Print information available on the last page.

iUniverse rev. date: 02/18/2016

Dedicated to all of my students, wherever they may be.

Lecture #1

(Given by the Political Science Department Chair)

Dr. A Will Make You Think

We are pleased to announce that Dr. Randy Arrington has graciously accepted an invitation from Chancellor Albert Carnesale to serve as a Visiting Professor in the department of political science at UCLA. But before Professor Arrington dives into the deep end on campus here in Westwood, we would first like to introduce him and offer some pertinent, biographical information. Perhaps after getting to know Dr. A's background you'll be more inclined to read his scholarly work. You might even be sufficiently motivated to engage him in some healthy, intellectual banter on the various topics introduced during his lively classroom discussions.

Randy Arrington is a retired Naval Aviator, who flew attack jets off the flight deck of four different aircraft carriers during his distinguished active duty and reserve Navy career. He was part of the expeditionary mission during the Iran Hostage Crisis, was awarded an Air Medal with Bronze Star for Meritorious Achievement in aerial flight, and rose to the rank of Commander during his 20 years of service.

He is also a retired U.S. Customs Interceptor Pilot who flew thousands of clandestine missions, fighting against American enemies in the War on Drugs and in the War on Terror. He served as Deputy Director of Air and Marine Operations in the San Diego Office for the Department of Homeland Security.

Dr. Arrington graduated from UCLA and went on to earn his PhD in political science from the University of New Orleans. As a professor he has taught numerous courses to both graduate and undergraduate students at Tulane, UCSD, USD, LSU, UNO, and now at UCLA.

Randy is author of the *Kerosene Cowboys* series of Naval Aviation action novels. The first book was successfully turned into a major motion picture entitled Red Sky.

He is also the proud father of five beautiful children.

Several of Dr. A's former students told us this: You did not have to agree with Dr. Arrington to get an A grade in his class. Most professors want to put their brain into your head. Dr. Arrington never did that to his students. What he did was motivate us to think, and to use the analytical part of our brain. He always spoke the truth. No lies, no deceptions, and no ideological propaganda were ever forced upon us. As students, we could argue for or against what he said, as he continuously engendered good, rational, intellectual discussions from all sides of each issue being considered. Every student in his classroom learned together and we were taught to appreciate, protect and respect each other's opinions while Dr. A was moderator of the discussion.

But be fully aware that being in the close proximity of Dr. Randy Arrington is NOT a safe space. You will be exposed to the Truth and he will endure the consequences.

Let Freedom Ring
God Help Us

Speak the Truth
Endure the Consequences

Welcome Randy Arrington, PhD

Lecture #2

James Madison Was Wrong

In *The Federalist Papers*, written in 1787-1788, James Madison, Alexander Hamilton and John Jay argued for ratification of our fledgling Constitution. Throughout this fine piece of political philosophy, Madison reassured the American people that our Federal government was not something to be frightened of. This new federal apparatus that had just been created by the Constitutional Convention in Philadelphia, would never deprive the states or individual citizens of their hard earned freedom. After all, the people would most assuredly elect men to federal office who were the best and brightest from among our population.

Well folks, James Madison was WRONG...!

An analysis of our electoral history reveals that quite often the American people have elected criminals, tyrants, buffoons and total incompetents to serve in office, primarily due to the overarching influence of campaign financing. A clear example of this is Barack Obama.

Less than 4 hours after it had begun, our CIA Station Chief in Benghazi informed President Obama that the consulate attack was a coordinated assault by al Qaeda. Armed with that crucial piece of information, Barack decided to go to bed and let the chips fall where they may in

Libya, because he had a long flight the next day to a fundraising event in Las Vegas.

But for the past 19 months, President Obama and his minions have flat out lied to the American people about the Benghazi Consulate attack and the murder for four brave citizens. It was merely a spontaneous, violent reaction to a YouTube video, they reassured.

As the damning evidence trickles out from his stonewalling, "transparent administration" it is now blatantly obvious that Barack Hussein Obama is the kind of man who is not only incompetent as a leader, but he is a man who is extremely comfortable engaging in a pattern of serial lies to camouflage his incompetence and his downright criminal behavior.

And he has grown accustomed to his lies being covered up by a vast array of conspiring individuals in our society, from the media, to the bureaucracy, to the public, to the courts, to his political party.

Bluntly stated, President Obama cannot be trusted and must be removed from office before he can inflict further damage on our nation.

Unfortunately, as brilliant as they were, the Founding Fathers didn't foresee that America would eventually have incredibly stupid people within the electorate. Ignorant parasites that are propagandized into believing they are victims, and who out of fear, would vote for a candidate that would supposedly give them a measure of temporary security in exchange for the surrender of their freedom.

These leech voters have chosen slavery over liberty. They have chosen involuntary servitude over freedom. Anyone who willingly gives up liberty in exchange for security deserves neither (Ben Franklin).

On the last day of the Constitutional Convention, a citizen asked Ben Franklin this question. What did you give us today Mr. Franklin? Ben replied, "A Republic, if you can keep it!"

Remember this folks; a Democratic Republic is always politically unstable, and requires constant nurturing to survive. It is never more than one generation away from total extinction.

Good men and women must boldly stand up and fight with courage and conviction for the preservation and continued longevity of America or it will vanish like a whisper in the wind.

Let Freedom Ring
God Help Us

Speak the Truth
Endure the Consequences

Randy Arrington, PhD

Lecture #3

Against All Enemies
Foreign and Domestic

Every American soldier, and every elected or appointed office holder in America takes a solemn oath to protect and defend The Constitution against ALL ENEMIES, both foreign and domestic. Based on their outlaw behavior, we have several elected and appointed officials in the Obama Administration who are NOT upholding their oath of office, and are in fact violating The Constitution on a weekly basis.

Unfortunately, many of our universities have been actively bombarding students with Marxist Communist ideology for over 50 years. Much to my dismay, Communism has finally made its way into The White House and into all branches of our government. Thus we now have transformed interpretations of our founding documents and diametrically opposed elucidations of the fundamental principles and values that have defined our nation since 1776.

Obama and his lawless regime constantly defile our Constitution, thus our president is a domestic enemy of the United States of America. The Senate under Harry Reid's non-leadership, hasn't passed a budget during the entire five and a half years that Obama has been president, thus Harry Reid is a domestic enemy of our nation as well. Every Member of The Senate and The House should be impeached and replaced with newly elected officials, to make a fresh start. The vast majority of these so-called political elites are not doing the jobs we elected them to do; they're merely protecting themselves to ensure re-election and the longevity of their own political power.

Politics and governing is NOT rocket science. Politics and governing is simple and it hasn't changed since Plato first wrote about it 2400 years ago in ancient Greece. If politics and governing is complex today it is because we have allowed it to become unnecessarily so.

Politics and governing is about who gets what, when and how. But that undergirding dynamic does not mean giving parasites a lifetime of entitlement, by stealing and redistributing the hard earned money of contributing citizens. The government's primary purpose is to protect individual liberty and provide national security. All of you freeloading, entitlement bloodsuckers should realize that when you suck the host organism dry, you die as well. As Maggie Thatcher used to say, Socialism NEVER WORKS, because eventually you run out of other people's money.

Our country is in dire jeopardy of collapse, and is quickly running out of time to be saved. We must protect The Constitution and our nation against the current assault, and it is our obligation as patriots to do so. The Declaration of Independence states that when government becomes destructive of the people's right to Life, Liberty and the Pursuit of Happiness, that it is the people's duty to alter or abolish that governing apparatus and to institute a new government that will be protective of those unalienable rights.

Unlike General Motors, America is NOT too big to fail, and I believe that we are currently living in pre-revolutionary times. The only ones capable of bailing us out are the good, productive citizens of America after they wake up and do the right thing and stop this madness.

Dr. Randy Arrington

I believe that an Article 5 Convention of the States will eventual happen, and it's a great vehicle from which to begin our national healing process.

Let Freedom Ring
God Help Us

Speak the Truth
Endure the Consequences

Randy Arrington, PhD

Lecture #4

(Given at Tulane University)

America Needs Leaders With Courage

When I teach political science at UCLA, I begin by postulating this humble premise to my students. Politics is simple. Politics is easy. In fact, the undergirding dynamic of politics hasn't changed since Plato and Aristotle were first conjuring up their political theories way back in ancient Greece.

Politics is the authoritative allocation of value in society. Simply stated, politics is about Who gets What, When and How. Value and values are disseminated from the myriad of resources we possess as a nation, both tangible and moral. Certainly our national assets are indeed abundant but they can be needlessly squandered unto extinction. There is a limit to what we can do with our national treasures.

Contemporary politics has evolved into a complex leviathan because we the people have allowed politicians and University Professors to deceive us into believing that politics is extremely complicated. And, as such, that it requires their particular brand of genius to comprehend and properly manage all of the intricate variables so that our society will be successful and have longevity. Power and prestige have indeed corrupted our politicians and our academics during this evolutionary process. There is no worse heresy than the office sanctifies the holder of it. But, again, we the people must share the blame.

The Founding Fathers created America as a nation based upon Locke's notion of consent of the governed (not divine right), and upon limited government intrusion to maintain order and liberty. Government was to protect the nation against invasion, both foreign and domestic, and to create an atmosphere of liberty. Freedom would encourage people to pursue opportunities to succeed in life, according to individual desires. As long as citizens didn't harm others during their pursuit of success and happiness, the government apparatus would not be an impediment to them. In other words, citizen's liberty would not be removed or incrementally chipped away by the government. Remember what Lord Acton taught us, liberty is not the power of doing what we like, but the right of being able to do what we ought to be doing.

Although Order, Freedom and Equality are the political goals that our American government pursues today, Equality in a social context didn't become a formally recognized objective in American society until Lincoln's Emancipation Proclamation. Economic Equality as a political value was solidified in the 1930's when Roosevelt's socialist public policy agenda was adopted.

In a society, Truth often Changes because truth is routinely subjected to human interpretation. What is highly valued in one generation can easily become the pariah of another. What is truth in one generation can easily become a lie in the hands of another.

Here is a good example: Hard work, ingenuity and determination are the pathway to success in America. Americans of our Greatest Generation understood this truth. They would literally pull themselves up by their bootstraps and work extra hard to become successful, despite the many obstacles thrown into their path.

This eternal truth slowly became distorted in the minds of progressives, liberal academics and socialist politicians, who successfully brainwashed activists, students and constituents into believing it to be a lie. Today many Americans believe that no amount of hard work will make them successful because the deck is unfairly stacked against their success. In fact, many believe that their continued failure in life is the direct result of a conscious conspiracy by some specified group of selfish, enterprising people.

Therefore the remedy for this unfair situation is that government must fully subsidize the failed citizen's existence, and forcibly deny liberty to those fortunate enough to be successful. The express purpose of socialists is to redistribute success and value to those among us who are allegedly less fortunate because of circumstances beyond their control.

In the 21st Century we do not have Majority Rules in America, as we were all taught in the fifth grade. Today, small cadres of people often dictate how the majority of citizens can and will live in society. Professor Brody at UCLA taught me that in America we have Minorities Rule. As such, we must continually be on guard because the "Tyranny of the Minority" is much worse and more damaging than the tyranny of the majority. The tyranny of the minority has the potential to permanently alter the way people actually think and analyze the political context in which they live.

To be sure, today's Socialist/Communist Democrats are a huge impediment to the longevity of contemporary American society, as envisioned by our Constitution. But there are others as well and they reside within the elite hierarchy of the Republican Party. Several elected officials and top organizational Republicans have deceived us into believing they are true conservatives. They are the Republicans in name only who, corrupted by the power and prestige of their office, do not have the courage to boldly stand up for conservative values. These elected officials sell out conservatism merely to get re-elected, and the leadership of the Republican Party allows this to occur during every campaign cycle. All of these individuals, these RINO'S need to be weeded out and sent back into private life. All of them need to be exposed for what they really are, and defeated at the polls or removed from those top echelons of the Republican Party organization.

When I was considering running for Congress in 2010 against Democrat Representative Susan Davis in California's 53 Congressional District, I was utterly dismayed by the attitude of the National Republican Congressional Committee (NRCC). The only question the NRCC asked me was how much money I could raise and how quickly. They claimed to like my true conservative political platform and my campaign motto (SPEAK THE TRUTH THEN ENDURE THE CONSEQUENCES). But when I told them that if I won the House seat I would only stay in office for three terms (six years) they turned a deaf ear to me. I told the NRCC that I would leave Congress and allow another individual to fill the office. After all, that's how The Founding Fathers envisioned public service in Congress; it was never intended to be a permanent, lifelong career as it is today. Remember this, where you have a concentration of power in a few hands, all too frequently men with the mentality of gangsters get control. History has proven that all power corrupts; absolute power corrupts absolutely (Lord Acton).

America needs strong leaders who will stand up and boldly speak the truth, despite the media onslaught and vitriol that will be hurled at them on a daily basis. This is a daunting task to ask of any potential statesman, but our nation is worth such a personal sacrifice. The danger is not that one class is unfit to govern. Every class is unfit to govern (Lord Acton).

Great men are almost always bad men. The conservatives that we elect must surround themselves with staffers who keep the office holder firmly grounded in humility, always reminding him or her that they are public servants, not rock star celebrities. The elected officials must never forget that the people they serve actually hold the power.

Elected representatives, merely exercise political power on behalf of their constituents. We all need to be a student of history because history is not a burden on the memory; it is an illumination of the soul (Lord Acton).

Let Freedom Ring
God Help Us

Speak the Truth
Endure the Consequences

Randy Arrington, PhD

Lecture #5

Runaway Train-Wreck Spending

Contemporary American Government has evolved into being nothing more than a cadre of well-dressed men and women gathering together in a pristine venue, to conjure up innovative new ways to steal people's hard-earned money. Then these aristocrat wannabes engage in demagoguery, fraud, fear mongering, smoke and mirrors, and outright lying in an attempt to justify their re-distributive tax and spend policies. This behavior has nothing whatsoever to do with politicians having compassion or an emotional attachment to certain groups of people. This conduct is solely for the selfish purpose of bolstering, protecting and expanding their own political power. Government calls it taxation but it is tantamount to de-criminalized robbery at the point of a political gun and/or targeted, veiled threats. If allowed to fester and continue unabated, this political dynamic will convey utter weakness to our enemies and ultimately destroy our nation from within. But our politicians don't really care about this probability. Politicians truly believe that they will be allowed to retain their vaunted, elite position at the top of our societal heap, in this New World Order. Machiavelli and *The Prince* would be so proud of them all.

These arrogant, drunk on power politicians DO NOT have a revenue problem. They have a huge spending problem. Trust me on this one subject class: Politicians are not smarter than us. They are not uniquely gifted to be politicians. They are public servants. I reiterate, all power corrupts and absolute power corrupts absolutely.

Consider these latest lunatic taxation ideas: A DRIVER'S MILEAGE TAX based on how many miles you drive each year because soon there will be huge numbers of electric or hybrid vehicles on the road. Or, newer model vehicles are getting increasingly more miles per gallon when driven. Because of this, governments at all levels will be collecting far less gasoline tax revenue.

A JOCK TAX because professional athletes who don't live in the cities where they routinely compete should be forced to pay those cities a tax while earning money in those locations.

Why can't the politician's understand that government doesn't have an income problem, government has a runaway, train-wreck spending problem?

Soon we will see A BREATHABLE AIR TAX based on a person's body size and lung capacity. How about A HEARTBEAT TAX, based on the number of heartbeats you have each year.

Government doesn't create anything except atmosphere and political context. Our government's sole purpose is to protect the nation from invasion (both foreign and domestic) and to secure individual liberty. As John Locke taught us in his 2nd *Treatise on Government*, when government abdicates this purpose, they quickly denigrate justification of their power and betray the fiduciary trust of the people they are elected to SERVE. Then the government eagerly begins the process of the destruction of individual liberty under the false guise of spreading equality to everybody in society. This alleged egalitarian government purpose inevitably leads to ultimate destruction of the sovereign nation and the individuals they are supposed to be protecting.

The American Revolution was fought and eventually won over the basic issue of NO TAXATION WITHOUT REPRESENTATION. Guess what people; we are NOT currently being represented by our elected politicians anymore. The politicians represent themselves and their lobbyist buddies who supply cash for re-elections campaigns. We are on a path of unsustainable spending and it will cause America to implode.

The ONLY way this type of runaway, train wreck spending can be sustained is for the government, at the business end of a gun, to confiscate ALL the wealth from everybody in America then redistribute it equally to every single person. This is called equality of outcome. This is called equality of poverty. This is called equality of misery. This is called equality of negative liberty. This is called COMMUNISIM.

Communism never works, NEVER EVER. Communism destroys individualism, imaginative innovation and personal initiative. Communism decimates nations and human beings. Obama and the group of progressive puppeteers that prop him up are indeed COMMUNISTS.

WE THE PEOPLE must rally and do everything that we can, within our power and within the boundaries of our laws, to defeat them all at the polls in the next two election cycles. This includes Republicans in name only, that are in actuality closet, big government progressives. There is no compromise.

All that is required for evil to triumph is for good men to do nothing (Edmund Burke).

Anybody who is willing to give up their precious liberty for some temporary security is deserving of neither (Ben Franklin).

Let Freedom Ring
God Help Us

Speak the Truth
Endure the Consequences

Randy Arrington, PhD

Lecture #6

American Mother's ROCK

Ever since the thirteen original British Colonies became a free nation on this continent, so-called scholars have argued over which variables elevated the United States of America into greatness, and its current superpower status. Some of the usual arguing points are: freedom, virtue, values, morals, capitalist economics, rational thought, politicians, government, religion, compassion, self-reliance, rugged individualism, incentive, ingenuity, determination, and military power.

I would like to argue that the undergirding foundation of American greatness incorporates each and every one of these important components into her basic character. American Mothers are a huge determining factor in our status and longevity as a great nation, and as we are nurtured into adulthood, our fabulous Moms deserve much more credit than they normally receive.

For instance:

Mom stands as a beacon of freedom as she gives us an umbrella of liberty, underneath which we can make all sorts of mistakes to learn from. She even lets us wear that Che Guevara T-Shirt in public then in private, teaches us the true facts about this ruthless, Communist Revolutionary.

Mom teaches us virtue when we are forced to admit we did not actually brush our teeth for bed but merely ran water over the toothbrush. If we ever lie to her again, she promises to wash our mouth out with lye soap.

Mom injects us with proper values when she makes us mow the lawn instead of playing video games on a Saturday afternoon. Then as a reward, she buys us the latest "Call to Duty" video game.

Mom shines as a pillar of morals by reminding us to be home by 11:00pm from our date, and is waiting patiently on the couch to monitor our arrival. She also listens as we attempt that first awkward kiss on the front porch.

Mom teaches us about capitalist economics as she argues with City Hall over our right to operate a lemonade stand on the sidewalk in front of our house. Liberal politicians want to have her arrested and carted off to jail, but they cower in reaction to her solid arguments at the Town Council meeting.

Mom engages in rational thought when she convinces our teacher that we deserve a better grade in English class. And, that she will not allow her children to participate in Common Core because of its mega-liberal bias.

Mom is a politician when she breaks up a sibling squabble then hands each of us a Klondike Bar. She forces her children to hug one another and apologize before handing them that delicious ice cream treat.

Mom governs us when we want to eat another Klondike bar instead of our broccoli at dinner. Sorry President Bush but broccoli is indeed good for us. Mom won't let us leave the table until we eat every last bite of it, or drop it down to the dog underneath our feet.

Mom fills us with religion every weekend at Church as our Sunday Schoolteacher. She also makes sure we are appropriately dressed to display respect for the church environment.

Mom shows us compassion when patching up a scraped knee from a biking accident in the driveway, or letting us cry on her shoulder after we break up with our significant other. She didn't really like that liberal punk we were dating anyway.

Mom teaches us self-reliance when she encourages us that we can indeed figure out that last math problem on our own. She also teaches us to wash, dry and fold our own dirty laundry.

Mom shows us how rugged individualism can help mold our character when she makes us walk those twelve long blocks to junior high school, always reminding us that her grandfather had to walk 5 miles to a one-room school house to receive his six years of education.

Mom instills incentive into us when she gives us an extra twenty bucks because we earned all A's on our most recent report card. She also reminds us of that B- we got last semester in Civics class. That will never happen again, we promised her.

Mom teaches us ingenuity by motivating us to be extra creative with our Science project. She buys all of the raw materials then watches diligently as we create a better mousetrap.

We learn determination from Mom when she helps us with batting practice until its dark outside, and then we get a single and a double in our next Little League game. After the ballgame she treats the entire team to smoothies, even our All Star girl pitcher.

Mom endorses military power as she pins a set of gold Naval Aviator Wings onto the left side of our white uniform shirt. The mere touch of her hand says she will catch us if ever we fall.

Dr. Randy Arrington

Many women give birth, but it takes a very special lady to be truly maternal.

A very Happy Mother's Day to all of you beautiful Moms out there in America.

Let Freedom Ring
God Help Us

Speak the Truth
Endure the Consequences

Randy Arrington, PhD

Lecture #7

Cultural Marxism & Political Correctness

Cultural Marxism is typically defined as the destructive criticism and undermining of all institutions of Western civilization and the traditional values underpinning it.

Convincing the parasites, the losers, and the weak-minded people in society that they are actually innocent victims in their plight is key to the success of *Cultural Marxism*. Once this psychological ideology infiltrates and totally possesses the requisite number of individuals within the masses, it becomes an unstoppable force for Communist Revolution.

First, so-called Communist Theorists identify a culprit causing the predicament of innocent, downtrodden people in the masses. Then the Communist Theorist promises that once they are entrusted with absolute power (political, military, judicial, media, educational, and economic), they will avenge those blameless, oppressed people in society by exacting an ultimate, well-deserved revenge against their nemesis.

But it is indeed a smokescreen, a facade, a deception, and a total lie. Once the Communists possess absolute power, they begin a reign of terror against ALL PEOPLE in the nation. The Communists brutally purge and murder millions of innocent individuals in order to instill a gripping, controlling fear within the masses. This means justifies their ends and solidifies their totalitarian control.

Cultural Marxism is the undergirding foundation that propels "Political Correctness" in American society today. Just after Lenin successfully completed his Communist Revolution in Russia, the ruling Bolsheviks created an institution called the Communist International, because they wholeheartedly believed Karl Marx who taught that the entire world would eventually transition to full blown Communism.

A critical component that would instigate this transformation to Communism was the annihilation of Western Christianity, which Antonio Gramsci theorized was the primary obstacle preventing a Communist New World Order. Gramsci argued that the Christian faith had tainted members of the working class in Western civilization and that the West would have to be de-Christianized through the obliteration of all traditional, Christian values and institutions. During their elongated trek through society, Communists would have to infiltrate and corrupt the traditional family, schools, churches, entertainment, media, civic organizations, science, literature and actually re-write human history.

Everything originating in Western civilization was to be attacked, ridiculed and mocked. Blame for all of the world's problems was to be assigned to the failings of Western culture and Capitalism. Through the construct of *Cultural Pessimism*, citizens would eventually begin to despise their own society, despite having experienced tremendous personal success. If a lie is repeated often enough it becomes the truth in many people's minds.

Instead of a disgruntled working class being the ultimate instigator of a Communist Revolution, marginalized groups would be the societal catalyst leading the way. Alienated groups like activist homosexuals, feminists, and black militants would use Political Correctness and Cultural Terrorism to wage war against white males, Christians, heterosexuals, capitalists and all things that were founded on traditional Western values and morals. Of course the so-called victim groups would be defended and exalted, as public debate was stifled and suffocated.

Does any of this sound familiar in contemporary American society?

Here is Dr. A's final analysis:

A Cultural Marxist is a human predator who preys upon weak-minded individuals. He is a "MIND RAPER" who culls out the worst in human nature, counting on intellectual poverty, to foment Communist Revolution. Don't let him get into your head.

In the long run, Communism NEVER WORKS. Communism ALWAYS FAILS in human society and it destroys the lives of everyone along the path to its eventual collapse.

But, good men and women still must boldly stand, face and aggressively defeat this Communist enemy. As Americans we must prevent the all-consuming misery that is ever-present in a temporary Communist Dictatorship. True, Conservative American Patriots will save our beloved nation.

In America, it is not only our right to question the government it is our duty to do so in order to protect our freedom and to ensure the continued, peaceful longevity of our Democratic Constitutional Republic.

The United States of America is indeed God's shining city set upon a hill.

Dr. Randy Arrington

We are the last, best hope for all mankind.

Let Freedom Ring.
God Help Us.

Speak the Truth.
Endure the Consequences.

Randy Arrington, PhD

Lecture #8

America in The Twilight Zone

I came to the surreal conclusion last night that we are living in THE TWILIGHT ZONE. Everything is now upside down with Barack Obama at the helm.

A shadowy, unknown, incompetent, community rabble rousing, Marxist Communist, effeminate man who admits to profusely using both marijuana and cocaine in his past becomes president. All while the liberally biased, mainstream media refuses to vet him but instead actively works to provide unprecedented levels of cover for him.

Obamacare is the single biggest domestic policy failure in American history, yet the Obama Administration spends billions of dollars to keep the program on a life-support machine.

A Commander in Chief who abrogates his responsibilities to our own soldiers with ridiculous Rules of Engagement during wartime, while ordering the illegal killing of American citizens in foreign countries with clandestine drone strikes.

A dangerously incompetent female Secretary of State who racks up unprecedented air miles all over the world, yet she has zero accomplishments and is now the presumed Democratic Presidential Nominee in 2016.

Illegal aliens are treated like proverbial royalty, while law-abiding American citizens are persecuted and/or thrown in jail without probable cause.

The IRS conspires with The White House to blatantly take away 1st Amendment free speech rights from targeted, conservative citizen groups then invokes the 5th Amendment when questioned by a Congressional Oversight Committee.

The DOJ conspires with The White House to take away American Citizen's 2nd Amendment gun rights, while at the same time freely supplying guns to vicious Mexican drug cartels.

Obama and Clinton keep our Libyan Consulate open despite huge threats of violence. They refuse to provide urgently requested increases in security then left four Americans to be murdered by Islamist terrorists. Then they deliberately lie about the heinous event to politically protect Obama during the re-election campaign. Yet during the phony sequester, they close and barricade the American people's precious national monuments, preventing our Veteran's and other citizens from visiting them.

Our government continuously lies to its own citizens, as our numerous Government agencies lie to each other within the bureaucracy merely to protect and increase their piece of the national budget pie.

When told about the various scandals that he and his administration have purposely made happen, Obama is: Outraged, Mad as Hell, It is Unacceptable, and he will Get to the Bottom of it. But he never gets to the bottom of anything except the cup on a putting green. Nobody is held accountable. Everything is swept under the political rug hoping ignorant people will forget ("Dude, that was like 2 years ago, What difference at this point does it make").

Homeland Security labels veterans, Christian groups and patriots as domestic terrorists, but Obama refused to call the Muslim, Fort Hood Mass murderer a terrorist.

Our tax dollars subsidize the annual Cowboy Poetry Festival in Harry Reid's Nevada while American Veterans are highly disrespected as our government shoves them to the back of every line and in fact places them on secret wait lists so that they are denied the benefits they have EARNED with their military service.

Students heed this statement: There can be no amateurs in politics because there are no professionals. By this I mean that everybody is an unqualified amateur and nobody should have power in a political context. But of course that is impossible within complex, human social relations.

In his *Allegory of the Cave*, Plato taught us that only philosophers could recognize, understand and properly use The Truth, therefore ONLY philosophers should rule as King. But even wise philosophical geniuses eventually become corrupted by the constant bombardment of political power.

All People are unqualified to lead inside the political arena. The best political leaders are those who do NOT really want to be a political leader but are forced to do so because of harsh circumstances in society.

When they are compelled to become leaders, these humble men and women will be much harder to corrupt inside the political realm, but they nonetheless must constantly be on guard against the overarching capacity of power to pervert their principles, ethics, morals and judgment.

In his seminal work *Leviathan*, Thomas Hobbes taught us that life was short, selfish, nasty and brutish, and that under the right circumstances, the weakest human being could kill the strongest. Therefore, human beings must have a huge, all-powerful government as part of their 'Social Contract' in order to keep people safely separated.

In his *Two Treatises on Government*, John Locke argued against Hobbes thesis. Locke wanted to use reason and tolerance to join human beings together under a government that was created through the Consent of the Governed, and not under the Divine Right concept of Monarchy. This was a highly revolutionary concept in 1689.

Barack Obama is indeed a Marxist who wants to fundamentally transform America into a Communist Totalitarian nation.

A totalitarian government "claims" they know exactly where the nation is heading. But they are ALWAYS WRONG.

A government based on Democratic principles does not know the inevitable destination of the society from day to day. They just provide a general roadmap and allow for detours along the pathway to national growth, maturity and longevity.

LIBERTY is the natural, God given craving for all of mankind. The desire for human freedom is relentless and although it can be temporarily repressed and forced to go dormant, it never dies in the human spirit.

Always remember this students: It is not only our right to question the government, it is our duty to do so in order to protect our freedom and to ensure the continued, peaceful longevity of our nation.

Let Freedom Ring
God Help Us

Speak the Truth
Endure the Consequences

Randy Arrington, PhD

Lecture #9

Memorial Day Honors

Memorial Day is not about a fancy car race in Indiana. It is not about a bunch of gay people strolling down the streets of San Francisco in unison. It is not about sleeping in for an extra couple of hours until it's time to get your family ready for that barbecue cookout on the charcoal grill in the backyard.

Memorial Day is when we pause and remember those brave men and women who have given the last full measure of allegiance to our nation. On Memorial Day we celebrate those heroic Americans who have lost their lives while protecting our freedom in this great country. Without their dedicated service and courageous sacrifice, our liberty would be severely curtailed by empires with evil designs against the people of the United States of America.

In military aviation when a pilot is killed, squadron mates fly a Missing Man Formation at the funeral service of the fallen hero. In the picture attached to this article, you'll notice that it is a four-plane wedge formation. But then just as the four jets arrive at the gravesite, one pilot pulls up and out of the wedge to create an obvious hole in this precision flight. The Missing Man Formation is flown in order to honor their lost squadron mate and to convey that they will always miss him or her and never forget the ultimate sacrifice that was made.

So the next time you see four military jets flying fast and low overhead, and one of them pulls up and out of the group to create the Missing

Man Formation; or if you see a picture of a bunch of M-16's stacked neatly in a row with a combat helmet on top of each rifle and a pair of combat boots on the ground in front of each weapon; or if you see a man tearing up at the Vietnam Memorial as he is using a pencil to etch the name of a fallen comrade onto a white sheet of paper, your heart should skip a beat as you recall those gallant heroes and the awful price they willingly paid to preserve your individual freedom and the American way of life.

So, on this Memorial Day as we fire up the charcoal in our Weber barbeque, tune in our television to watch that fancy car race in Indiana, and just relax and enjoy this Holiday, American hearts should feel a bit heavy as we remember and commemorate our brave military men and women and the awful price they willingly paid to preserve our way of life.

Freedom is not free and the proverbial tree of liberty must be refreshed from time to time with the blood of both patriots and tyrants.

LADIES AND GENTLEMEN, I HUMBLY SALUTE YOU......!

Let Freedom Ring
God Help Us

Speak the Truth
Endure the Consequences

Randy Arrington, PhD

Lecture #10

Presidential Eras and Presidential Power

Writing in *Federalist #70*, Alexander Hamilton argued that the fledgling United States of America desperately needed a president.

But over the last 225 years, many so-called scholars have demonstrated that the American presidency, while being a unique and necessary political construct, is also an inherently dangerous paradigm as well.

Thus we have the logical paradox of the American presidency.

America needs a president but the power of that office is always a potential threat to our individual liberty as citizens.

Likewise, the appropriate use of political power and leadership has always been a perplexing one, in part because of the sustaining myth that the people are sovereign (Cronin and Genovese).

Alexis de Tocqueville (*Democracy in America*) captured this puzzling aspect of American political life when he said that "the people want to be led and they want to remain free.

Since they cannot destroy ether of these contradictory propositions, the Americans strive to satisfy them both at once through democratic constitutional government."

Thus we have the logical paradox of the American people.

Bearing this in mind, F. Scott Fitzgerald taught us that the ultimate trial of a truly intelligent human being is the ability to embrace two diametrically opposed concepts, simultaneously in their mind, without going insane.

When I teach The American Presidency course at UCLA, I always begin by introducing my students to a modern concept of presidential power known as the Three Eras of the Presidency.

This analytical design is a standard diagnostic tool used by presidential analysts to examine American Presidents.

Discovering how each Chief Executive used or abused the enumerated and inherent powers of their office and what success or failure they engendered, is one of the purposes of using this construct.

Determining who are the great presidents and who are the failed presidents is another goal.

The Three Eras of the American presidency are:

> The Heroic Era
> The Imperial Era
> The Post-Imperial Era.

During the Heroic Era, several authors glorified the men of the presidency.

Men like Washington, Lincoln, Jefferson, Jackson, Roosevelt, Wilson and Truman were worshiped as the great presidents.

Academics such as Clinton Rossiter (*The American Presidency*) called the presidency "the office of freedom."

He viewed it as the exact opposite of tyranny and "the office that helps ordinary citizens realize their hopes and dreams.

Power has never corrupted the presidency....EVER...!

Why, because the men who have held the office knew that their vast powers came from the people, and they respected this fact."

During the Heroic Era, presidential power was good.

In the 1970's, presidential researchers offered us a profoundly different conception of the American presidency, probably due to the bad taste in their mouth stemming from the Vietnam War and Watergate scandal.

During the Imperial Era of the presidency journalists and authors characterized the office as the American monarchy.

In his book *The Twilight of the Presidency*, George Reedy argued "far from ennobling its occupants, the office creates an environment in which presidents cannot function in any kind of decent and human relationship with the people they are supposed to lead."

Presidential advisers were most to blame in this situation because they never wanted to tell the chief Executive any bad news.

These sycophants merely told the president what they wanted to hear, quickly becoming *Victims of Groupthink* (Janus Irving).

As such, they purposely isolated the Chief Executive from the harsh realities of political life.

Depraved presidential decisions were often the result of this isolation.

During the Imperial Era of the presidency, presidential power was bad.

From 1961 through 1978, our nation had five different presidents and a relatively rapid turnover of executive power.

This caused the presidents to have a rapid style of policymaking and witnessed them engaging in politically risky activities merely to get elected.

During the campaign, candidates tended to unrealistically raise hopes among the electorate about what they would do and accomplish once in office.

During the Post-Imperial Era, presidents cut corners and quickly hammered legislation through Congress, leaving the details of implementation to members of the unelected bureaucracy (Cronin and Genovese).

This approach to governing from The White House proved disastrous on numerous occasions because presidential power had been thoroughly weakened.

During the Post-Imperial Era, presidential power was debilitated.

I argue that with Barack Obama at the helm, we are currently suffering through the Fourth Era of The American Presidency.

The Rogue Era

The Rogue Era is characterized by unrepentant lawlessness on the part of the president and his administration.

The Constitution is not the law of the land, it is merely and ancient document that serves as a guideline for action.

Therefore, all of our sacred founding documents are to be constantly re-interpreted by Ivy League lawyers and relentlessly spun by the media to coincide with the political path the Chief Executive has chosen for America.

During the Rogue Era, presidential power is destructive.

This is the most hazardous time for America in our entire, glorious history.

If We the People don't seize the unbridled, lawless, unconstitutional power away from Obama or any other Communist Democrat who occupies the Office of the President, our nation WILL COLLAPSE and be totally dismantled and destroyed forever.

Today is the 70th anniversary of D-Day.

All true, patriotic Americans (past, present and future) were at Normandy on June 6, 1944.

I do not believe for one second that those brave men who stormed the beaches of France to bring an end to World War II and who willingly sacrificed their lives for American liberty did this so that a man like Barack Obama would be put into The White House by ignorant, parasitic voters who do not understand the danger in trading their sovereignty and freedom for some temporary material security.

Remember, American Liberty is ALWAYS just one generation away from extinction (Ronald Reagan).

There can be no patriotism without liberty; no liberty without virtue; no virtue without citizens (Rousseau).

Let Freedom Ring
God Help Us

Speak the Truth
Endure the Consequences

Randy Arrington, PhD

Lecture #11

Eulogy for a Submarine Sailor

Children of submarine sailors tell different stories than other kids do. None of our fathers can teach a history class, speculate on a stock, write a song, make Veal Parmesan, sink a hole-in-one, preach the gospel, cut hair, give a tetanus shot, analyze Marxist Theory, or describe the theme of a Hemingway novel.

We tell of fathers who go out on secret submarine patrol, remaining submerged for six months, during which the position of the ship is not known once it leaves the Naval Base. Our fathers sailed underneath the polar ice cap, launched Ballistic Missiles, fired torpedoes, dived down to a few feet above crush depth, and spied on enemy nations.

Your Dads coached football, sold cars, taught mathematics, prosecuted criminals, ran a barbershop, and were real estate tycoons. You don't like war, or violence, or nuclear tipped torpedoes, or napalm, or depth charges, or cruise missiles.

We were raised by men who made America the most secure nation on earth. We grew up attending Memorial Services for submarine sailors who were lost at sea in ships like Thresher and Scorpion. Your fathers made local communities decent, prosperous, growing and functional. Our fathers made the world safe for democracy.

We have gathered here today to celebrate the remarkable and storied life of John Arrington, who was simply called "Jackie" by his Mother early on in his life that began about 84 years ago in Oklahoma.

Although this day is filled with sorrow, we can take great comfort in knowing that my Dad lived a wonderful life. Always at full speed ahead. Sometimes it seemed like he was running around as if his hair was on fire and his rear end was catching.

John Arrington didn't know what temperance was, or mediocrity, or where you would go to find these things. As such, his self-esteem was absolutely indisputable, but he wasn't arrogant or pompous. His was an assured self-confidence, and it was one of his most endearing qualities.

From the first day you met my Dad, you knew you were in the presence of greatness. You quickly realized that his contagious smile could immediately light up any room, rendering even the most stubborn people helpless to defend against his cheerful demeanor and positive attitude.

My Dad adored his wife and cherished his children. He wished everyone could be just like him, a strapping, dark haired, matinee idol. I would bet that he hadn't spent more than a few thousand dollars in his whole life on a wardrobe, with the possible exception of a closet full of cowboy shirts and Lee jeans.

John Arrington is a true American Hero. His life was filled with the kinds or things that screen writers extol in their scripts, but movie directors can never adequately capture up on the big screen, precisely because it was reality not fantasy.

My Dad served with honor and great distinction for 20 years as a submarine Chief Petty Officer in the US Navy. As a member of our Greatest Generation, he protected America and kept us safe from the numerous threats to national security that existed in the mid 40's through the mid 60's. After his military retirement, he worked in the motion picture industry for over 30 years, helping to produce a variety of entertainment that we have all enjoyed on television and in movie theaters.

My remarks here today are intended to paint a snapshot of my Dad's professional experience. The words have been choreographed so that all of us can derive a sense of what it was like to live the kind of life that he was privileged to lead.

John Arrington was a 20th Century *Kerosene Cowboy*, riding a bucking bronco in the rodeo of his two chosen professions. But his bronc wasn't made of hair and hoof. It was made of metal and wires, carbon fiber and glass, torpedoes and missiles, generators and spotlights, cameras and sound stages. And my Dad always rode for the full 8 seconds, every time out of the chute, whether he was submerged in a submarine, or on a movie set in Hollywood.

My Dad was a Submarine Sailor at heart, but he also loved being a motion picture man, and he was exceptionally gifted at both. John Arrington was a man's man. He lived a great life, always doing what he loved to do. Going out to sea, defending America. Working long hours at the movie studio to finish a film. Spending quality time with family. Joking with friends and coworkers. Every one of us should be so lucky.

Here is how my father appeared to me as a boy. He came from a race of giants, out of a mythical land known as Tulsa. He married the most beautiful girl ever to sashay out of Colombia, Mississippi. There were times when I thought we were being raised by Zeus and Athena.

After work and Happy Hour my father would race his car home to see his wife, children and puppy dog. He would get out of his car, a handsome, hulk of a man, and walk toward his house. His knuckles dragging along the ground, his shoes stepping on and killing small rodents as he ambled toward his home.

Some of the best times were when my Dad grabbed his catcher's mitt and took my brother and I to the playground for a game of catch. Or when he took out his set of golf clubs, dusted them off then drove us to the local golf course to play 18 holes.

During the Cuban Missile Crisis, my mother took me out to the New London Naval Base where we watched Dad's submarine sail silently and majestically out of the channel into the dark water of the Atlantic Ocean. We stood not more than thirty feet from the spot where the submarine sailors had barbequed steaks and boiled corn on the cob for a family picnic the week before.

My Dad was always a protector, who would fight for those who couldn't defend themselves against tyranny both foreign and domestic. I recall when he turned off all of the electricity at Hollywood General Studios until Francis Ford Coppola finally paid every member of the crew who were working on his latest film, and yet hadn't received a paycheck in over four weeks for their work.

Dad also introduced a new dynamic to LA Dodgers baseball games. John Arrington and his family would always arrive early to Dodger Stadium, where we watched the entire game and then left the ballpark late to avoid freeway traffic.

My Dad's wit was stunning; His intellect impressive; His humor infectious; His heart massive.

Mom, we all love you and we all love Dad. We will all miss him. We are all better people for having him touch our lives. And, we all look forward to being reunited with him in Heaven.

Dr. Randy Arrington

Dad, you were one helluva good man. I am so honored and proud to be your son.

Ladies and gentlemen please remember to Honor your Dad on Father's Day. We only have them in our lives for a brief period of time.

Let Freedom Ring
God Help Us

Speak the Truth
Endure the Consequences

Randy Arrington, PhD

(Modeled after *Eulogy for a Fighter Pilot* by Pat Conroy)

Lecture #12

Five Branches of Federal Government

On the 4th of March 1789 the Constitution of the Untied States of America formally went into effect, after first being ratified by the thirteen sovereign states.

In this document, the Founding Fathers created three branches of Federal Government, outlining all of the various constraints and limitations on the enumerated powers that these governing bodies would possess and use as they governed our fledgling nation.

But since 1932, these three branches of Federal Government have morphed into five branches of Federal Government: the Legislative, the Executive, the Judiciary, the Bureaucracy, and the Media. This transformation has not been a positive outcome, and in its current form it does not bode well for the continued, peaceful longevity of America.

Today, the Legislative Branch of our federal government has evolved into a bunch of lazy millionaires in both houses of Congress. These elected, so-called elites don't even write or read proposed laws anymore. The majority of the members of Congress merely wait on draft bills to be handed down to them from the Executive Branch. These pieces of legislation are usually written by political activists and professional lobbyists. The new modus operandi for sitting Members of Congress is simply to engage in pompous displays of delay and amendment with regard to governing and problem solving. Of course Senators and Representatives spend a great amount of their time doing TV interviews for their adoring media cohorts and being fawned over by various activist groups that have similar ideological views. Their only true purpose is to do whatever is required to ensure their own re-election.

Most Senators and Representatives have never held a job for any significant length of time outside the political arena, they do not truly care about solving national problems, and they literally loathe the people in their constituency because they are forced to interact and pander to these "commoners" during their re-election campaign.

The Executive Branch, with Barack Obama at the helm, is now a dictatorship engaged in soft tyranny turning quickly towards hard, entrenched despotism. The Chief Executive sets the legislative agenda for Congress during his State of the Union speech. Later, when he doesn't get what he wants, President Obama simply bypasses Congress by making passionate appeals to his voting base, denigrating the political adversaries on his enemies list, and through the use of and endless array of Executive Orders, most of which are illegal and in direct violation of our Constitution.

Obama and his supportive minions then offer an unlimited amount of lies, political spin and propaganda to confuse people and cover the president's tracks. Machiavelli would be so proud of Obama.

Our Judicial Branch has turned from upholding our Constitution into a highly partisan, activist body that actually makes laws using judicial activism, adhering vehemently to their personal agenda and political ideology. The Federal Courts System has very little to do with the dissemination of actual justice; it is now focused on social justice, a term that emanates from Cultural Marxism.

The Fourth Branch of our government is the mammoth, Leviathan Federal Bureaucracy. German sociologist Max Weber taught us that the Bureaucracy is where the real power exists in any government. These faceless, nameless, unelected entities can exercise overwhelming power and totally control people through their ability to write rules and regulations that have the impact of law. The Bureaucracy is also the formal apparatus of government where laws are implemented and enforced on society.

The Fifth Branch of our Federal Government is the mega-liberal, compliant, mainstream media. No longer is the American media a watchdog for the people. Today's mainstream media actively protects and promotes Obama's Socialist/Communist political agenda as it attempts to brainwash people into compliance. The mainstream media employs powerful propaganda tactics against the weak minded, the losers, and the parasites that constitute an ever-increasing portion of our society.

If they were united, the sovereign states and individual citizens could easily defeat this federal tyranny by decapitating the five-headed Hydra.

The undergirding source of all federal power is not the Constitution; it is the seemingly unlimited supply of money stolen from hard working American citizens, businesses and states that actually gives power to the Federal Government.

Of course this larceny is accomplished through the use of legalized extortion schemes called Federal Taxes, which includes innovative and invasive taxation of all kinds that is designed to steal our individual liberty and provide the Federal Government with its undergirding source of power.

One day when the majority of the good, hard working, contributing citizens of the USA finally wake up and realize that our Federal Government has made a hard left turn toward Socialist/Communist political policies, a tax revolt will commence. This tax revolt, and the resultant withholding of money from the Federal Government will quickly remove the unbridled power away from the governing apparatus in Washington, DC and put that authority back into the hands of it's rightful, legitimate owners, the citizens.

In the not too distant future, true American patriots are going to be forced by the magnitude of circumstances to develop a ruthless resolve as a nation.

When that fateful day finally arrives, we will begin to treat people (domestic and foreign) who want to destroy our country in the callous and coldblooded fashion they deserve.

America's ultimate survival depends on developing this style of brutal behavior at least until the scourge of the Communist threat (whether from foreign or domestic enemies) subsides and we can return to the normalcy of our peaceful, "sleeping giant" syndrome once again.

Unfortunately, today is not that day but I envision that it is looming out there on the horizon for our great nation.

Let Freedom Ring
God Help Us

Speak the Truth
Endure the Consequences

Randy Arrington, PhD

Lecture #13

Liberalism and the Transformation of America to Communism

On this 4TH of July, most Americans will gather with their family and friends around a barbeque grill and a picnic table to celebrate the birth of our nation.

As we commemorate the creation of America, and watch the fireworks displays in our hometowns, let us reflect on that bold decision to throw off the shackles of British tyranny some 238 years ago, and then assess where we stand as a free nation today.

Our Founding Fathers, brilliant yet likewise flawed men, were avid followers of John Locke and his political philosophy as outlined in *Two Treatises of Government*.

Typically referred to as the Father of Modern Liberalism, Locke introduced *rational reasoning* as the basis for invention of government, evolving out of the chaos and anarchy that characterized the proverbial State of Nature.

Locke postulated that establishing a governing authority was no longer the King's God-Given right to be Monarch.

As such, he replaced the traditional concept of *Divine Right* to govern with his theory of *Consent of the Governed*.

In Lockean political philosophy, only the sovereign people possess rights.

The government has only duties that it is obligated to fulfill for the people who first formed it.

This was of course viewed as revolutionary political thought in the 17th and 18th Centuries.

In drafting The Declaration of Independence, Thomas Jefferson used several of Locke's revolutionary hypotheses.

He even expressed his Americanized version of Locke's theory of *justified rebellion* in his famous phrase, "the tree of liberty must be refreshed from time to time with the blood of patriots and tyrants."

Combined with the Constitution, these two founding documents fashioned the formal charter of our fledgling government apparatus.

And they did so from a Modern Liberal perspective.

This newly founded Law of the Land included these Lockean (Modern Liberal) theories:

Limited government; Inalienable individual rights; Inviolability of property rights; The right of the people (as both Trustor and Beneficiary) to replace any government (as Trustee) if it violates the *fiduciary trust* it has been granted by their sovereignty.

These innovative ideas were integral to the birth and continued longevity of our nation.

But our Founding Fathers were also keenly aware of the possibility that wicked men would purposely attempt to subvert these precepts to further their own selfish desires as the nation moved forward. And as our nation matured, these fears have been justified on numerous occasions.

Modern (Classic) Liberalism was indeed the undergirding, philosophical foundation that the Founding Fathers used to build our nation.

In the late Eighteenth Century, Classic Liberal political philosophy (taught by both Montesquieu and Locke) meant unwavering defense of individual freedom, consent of the governed, limited government, restraint on government through the separation of powers doctrine, justified rebellion, and steadfast defense of capitalism as the most viable economic system.

Professor William Ebenstein taught me that "underlying Montesquieu's *separation of powers* doctrine was the unstated premise of a *negative state*, the state that was primarily a night watchman, maintaining law and order, and protecting the liberty of property and freedom of the individual.

As Liberalism, since the early 20th Century, became increasingly oriented toward the *positive state*, the state of broadened scope and enlarged activity, the separation of powers doctrine lost its appeal" with many wicked, selfish for power (William Ebenstein), American politicians and likewise among parasitic, entitlement citizens with limited capabilities who possess no work ethic.

As such, since the beginning of the 20th Century, Classic Modern Liberalism has been totally and irretrievably transformed in a systematic fashion by so-called Progressives, to further their own selfish, clandestine, socialist interests.

Ludwig von Mises succinctly captured this total transformation in his book *Liberalism in the Classical Tradition*:

"Today in the United States, liberal means a set of ideas and political postulates that in every regard are the opposite of all that liberalism meant to the preceding generations. The American self-styled liberal aims at government omnipotence, is a resolute foe of free enterprise, and advocates all-around planning by the authorities. Every liberal policy is aimed at confiscating some of the assets of those who own more than the average or at restricting the rights of property owners. Today, these concepts are considered liberal and progressive."

I argue that in contemporary America, Liberalism is now merely the new, toned down, politically correct name for Communism and Cultural Marxism.

Today, Liberals are indeed Communists in every way that Karl Marx first prescribed for them to behave in *The Communist Manifesto*.

To reiterate, we can blame the Progressives for this transformation. Teddy Roosevelt, Franklin Roosevelt and Woodrow Wilson started and perpetuated this ugly transformation of Liberalism as it evolved into Marxist Communism in America.

FDR perfected the transformation when he convinced progressives to refer to themselves as Liberals, to mask their true Communist intentions or America.

I will never support any politician or member of our government that is actively trying to transform America into a Marxist Communist society.

Neither should you because Communism NEVER works........!

When will Progressive Liberals realize the ignorance of their ways?

Probably never.

Let Freedom Ring
God Help Us

Speak the Truth
Endure the Consequences

Randy Arrington, PhD

Lecture #14

The "Chain-Link" Theory of the American Collapse

Barack Hussein Obama is indeed incompetent when viewed from the perspective of an American politician who reveres our Constitution, protects our individual Liberty, respects our traditions and moral values, nurtures our dominant political culture, promotes our capitalist economic system and fears God. From his first day in office, Obama has done none of this. In fact he and his administration work every single day to destroy each of these basic, guiding principles of our society and to actively foment anarchy and chaos within our nation.

Viewed from the perspective of a Marxist Communist revolutionary, Barack Obama is highly competent. He has purposely dragged America closer to destruction and collapse and into a Communist transformation more than any other clandestine Marxist has ever achieved. Trust me on this one subject. You will not enjoy living in a Communist society because the only way Marxism works for a brief period of time is for the government to brutally murder millions of innocent people. They do this to inject total fear into the masses in order to control their every action 24 hours a day.

From an analytical perspective, this is what I see happening in the United States of America at this very moment. It is a diabolical process of national destruction being perpetrated by the Radical Left that actually began to take shape incrementally during the Woodrow Wilson administration.

The United States of America is currently going through the initial phases of a Socialist Communist Revolution, straight out of the playbook of Marxist Theory, and its occurring right before our very noses people. Therefore, I humbly present for your consideration **The "Chain-Link" Theory of the American Collapse**. Individually, each of these links in the Communist Revolutionary chain could not achieve the goal. But when simultaneously combined together, the objective of a Communist transformation is suddenly within reach of the Marxist architects who are clandestinely orchestrating it.

This is how you would proceed if you were purposely attempting to fundamentally change our society and destroy America. See if it raises an alarm bell in you like it has in me. We still have the power to stop and reverse this process, but the time grows short. The next two elections are integral to reversing this Communist Revolution before its too late. Good men and women must act to stop the collapse of America.

The "Chain-Link" Theory of the American Collapse

1. Gut the military and the national defense industry so that our nation is weak and highly vulnerable to enemy attack and invasion. Purge most of the senior military leaders and replace them with incompetent puppets of the regime. Create a rival, armed civilian military/police force, to do the bidding of the Dictator without question.

2. Collapse the capitalist economy with runaway train-wreck spending, extreme unemployment, and devalue the currency so it becomes worthless. Make a majority of people totally

dependent on the government apparatus for every aspect of their daily existence. This leads to internal implosion of society.

3. Encourage class and race warfare, creating extreme civil unrest. Play the Blame Game and identify an internal enemy as the villain responsible for the misery and failure of the have-nots in society. Encourage and sponsor anarchy and chaos then offer tyranny as the only viable solution to our national security and longevity. The majority then allows tyranny to flourish and liberty to vanish.

4. Obliterate all borders. Encourage and allow everyone to enter the nation with impunity.

5. Devaluation of the English language with sponsored proliferation of numerous languages as acceptable communication alternatives. Do not formally identify English as our national language and engage in the wholehearted embrace of a diversity of languages.

6. Devaluation of traditional American Culture in preference to extreme diversity. Cultural Warfare also includes destruction of the traditional American family and our family values. Government becomes an advocate of moral decay in society. Discredit the undergirding national culture in favor of extreme diversity and nationalities of all kinds as being equal or superior to our own culture.

7. Discredit the founding documents and the Founding Fathers of our nation using the courts system as your agent of criticism. Devalue and ultimately destroy our Constitution and Declaration of Independence. Promote and allow Cultural Marxism and Political Correctness to permeate our society, thus controlling the behavior and thought process of Americans.

8. Attack and devalue Christianity, the Christian religion, its fundamental precepts and icons like Jesus Christ, Christmas and Christmas trees, and religion in general. Promote atheism.

9. Facilitation of politically expedient and politically sponsored corruption. Create a domestic spy network to monitor all citizens then put dissidents in jail for crimes against the state. Later have "show trials" and public executions. Our current DOJ, IRS, NSA and DHS have turned into highly corrupt political bureaucracies.

10. Control of communication and the dissemination of information to include overt repression of the truth and overt proliferation of false propaganda. Hijack the media.

11. Strict control of transportation and energy production.

12. Infiltrate then control the education system and use Marxist propaganda as the undergirding foundation of teaching students about everything.

13. Good men and good women do nothing to stop the destruction.

All of these links in the chain of an American collapse renders our nation overly ripe for national destruction due to internal implosion, which is exactly how Karl Marx predicted that a Communist Revolution would ensue. Obama has done all of these things because it's all part of his plan and straight out of the Saul Alinsky, Communist Revolution playbook.

COMMUNISM NEVER WORKS (It only works in the faculty lounge or the lecture halls of a University).

COMMUNISM ALWAYS FAILS (People are robbed of their incentive and innovation).

Dr. Randy Arrington

COMMUNIST CITIZENS LIVE IN ABJECT POVERTY AND
TOTAL MISERY (Except for the leaders of the Communist Party).

Wake up America before we no longer have the ability to stop this
collapse of our beloved United States of America. We must elect TRUE
CONSERVATIVES during the next two elections. This of course,
would represent only the first step in saving our beloved nation and
restoring our society's greatness.

I predict that good men and women will stand up to fight and ultimately
save the United States of America from collapse. But the blood of both
patriots and tyrants will be spilled into the streets and neighborhoods
of America in order to refresh our Tree of liberty.

Let Freedom Ring
God Help Us

Speak the Truth
Endure the Consequences

Randy Arrington, PhD

Lecture #15

Beware the Rattlesnake Obama

Despite the historic Mid-Term election of 2014 that swept a wave of new conservative politicians into office at all levels of government in America, the next twenty four months will be the most consequential and dangerous of times for us as a freedom loving, Constitutional Republic.

When you have a rattlesnake trapped in a corner, the deadly viper will not surrender. Instead, the serpent will come out aggressively fighting until it is killed or it kills you.

You don't realize it yet, but during the next two years in America we will be fighting in the final political battle that will ultimately determine the fate and longevity of the USA as a free nation.

Right now, Obama and his Communist minions are actively planning and setting numerous political traps for Conservatives.

And if the Republicans prove yet again to be ignorant, naive or weak, Obama will crush them and successfully transform the nation to Marxist Communism.

As usual, the Democrat Communists will use the ignorance and alleged despair of the loser parasites in the electorate, or soon to be in the electorate, combined with the callow hubris of the RINO Conservatives to complete the job.

And the mainstream media will provide an abundance of cover for these heinous activities.

IF Republicans courageously stand up and energetically thwart Obama at every turn without flinching, members of the President's own political party will eventually introduce The Articles of Impeachment against Obama.

And it will be the Democrats themselves who will cast the key votes to remove him from office. They will do this just to save a modicum of power for the remnants of their own political party.

By the way, I DO NOT trust Boehner or McConnell or McCain or the so-called Republican establishment.

These RINO knuckleheads will have to be dragged kicking and screaming across the finish line, in the pivotal race to save America from Obama and the Marxist Communists who want to destroy our nation.

We The People have the ultimate power to compel the politicians to do the right thing and save America.

But we must be actively and aggressively engaged in the political process at every step of the way.

Wake Up People.
It's Our Choice.

Let Freedom Ring
God Help Us

Speak the Truth
Endure the Consequences

Randy Arrington, PhD

Lecture #16

Our University System and the Future of America

Over the past 100 years or so, our university system has slowly evolved away from being an honored venue of higher learning and encouragement of a rational, analytical thought process, into being a methodical, diabolical, Communist brainwashing machine.

On campus, our university students are bombarded daily with a bitter, upside down concept of social justice, a warped sense of entitlement and an overarching notion of so-called political correctness.

All of these socially engineered concepts are fundamental principles contained within *Cultural Marxism,* a movement first created by Vladimir Lenin because he truly believed in the political philosophy of Karl Marx who taught that the entire world would eventually transition to full blown Communism.

Cultural Marxism is typically defined as the destructive criticism and undermining of all institutions of Western civilization and the traditional values upon which it is built.

To quickly achieve the goal of world domination, Lenin argued that the Communists would have to infiltrate and corrupt the traditional family, schools, churches, entertainment, media, civic organizations, science, literature and actually re-write human history.

In Lenin's plan, everything about Western civilization was to be endlessly attacked, mocked and ridiculed, and the ultimate blame for every dilemma confronting mankind was to be assigned to the failings of Western culture and Capitalism.

In American society today, Cultural Marxism is indeed the undergirding foundation that propels political correctness, social justice and the entitlement mentality.

I witnessed this first hand as a political science professor at UCLA (my alma mater), during classroom discussions, campus protests, faculty lounge conversations and even in the grading process.

For instance, I always graded research papers based on content, theme, progression, continuity, proper grammar, and writing style.

To me it didn't really matter which side of the political continuum my students adopted in their writing, so long as they presented sound arguments from their individual perspective.

And, as their professor, I never allowed my students to know where my personal sentiments lay along that Liberal/Conservative political spectrum.

Over the years, I received a few personal threats from disgruntled, entitlement mentality students if I didn't give them a higher grade.

I likewise received a few horrible professor reviews, probably from those same disgruntled students.

But, I NEVER changed a grade as a result of a personal threat or a bad review.

And I always taught my university students THE TRUTH, no matter how rude or out of touch it was perceived to be by them, due to the inculcation of Cultural Marxism they had received from other so-called scholars.

Today, most professors are mega-liberal and want to indoctrinate their students into accepting Cultural Marxism and a Communist utopian view of ordering society.

They literally want to put their brain into the heads of their students and create Communist robots.

I offered my university students the truth, the whole truth and nothing but the truth, then encouraged them to think analytically for themselves, in order to discover if I was actually telling them the truth.

Motivating our college students to think analytically, using a rational thought process, is and should be a core fundamental of higher learning.

And we desperately need to return to this basic, philosophical foundation in our universities before it's too late and our nation is destroyed by a Communist transformation.

Jesus Christ warned his followers that they would be persecuted for their belief in Him.

As such, they would have to fight to preserve their Christian faith because it would be under constant assault and in jeopardy of fading away or being forcibly taken from them.

Similarly, the Founding Fathers warned patriotic citizens that their individual liberty and the longevity of the newly created Democratic Constitutional Republic could be fleeting entities.

Both would be under constant assault by tyrants whose ambition would be to steal personal freedom, destroy the American political system and enslave human beings.

Remember, our democratic form of government is always just one generation away from extinction, and this is precisely why patriotic American citizens must be vigilant and constantly struggle to preserve our beloved nation and our sacred, individual liberty.

Communism ALWAYS FAILS and it eviscerates the lives of everyone along the path to its own inevitable collapse, but good men and women still must boldly stand, face and aggressively defeat this Communist enemy.

As true American Patriots we must prevent the all-consuming misery that infiltrates a nation during a temporary Communist Dictatorship.

Remember, in America it is not only our right to question authority and government actions, it is our duty to do so.

We actively monitor and query our own government to protect our freedom and to ensure the continued, peaceful longevity of our Democratic Constitutional Republic.

I truly believe that America is God's shining city set upon a hill for all to see.

We are the last, best hope for all mankind.

Let Freedom Ring
God Help Us

Speak the Truth
Endure the Consequences

Randy Arrington, PhD

Lecture #17

World War III and the Islamo-Communist

As millions of good people in France are demonstrating against Radical Islam, it is high time for all of us to boldly Speak the Truth then Endure the Consequences here in the United States of America.

Trust me on this one subject people, we are currently engaged in World War III, but the vast majority of Americans don't realize it or just want to downplay reality using the political correctness tactics contained in Cultural Marxism.

It is clear that America has no leadership at the helm, when viewed from a traditional, Capitalist, Democratic, Constitutional Republic perspective, and our Founding Fathers would be literally appalled at what they would see today in contemporary America.

Barack Obama's conspicuous absence from the anti-Muslim Jihadist rally of national leaders yesterday in Paris speaks volumes to the world that he is a total embarrassment and a miserable failure as an American President.

Apparently he was too busy preparing to prosecute a true America hero, General David Petraeus, and getting ready to greet the San Antonio Spurs in The White House Rose Garden.

I wouldn't be the least bit surprised if Obama sent the Statue of Liberty back to Jacques Chirac, then after reading the newspapers he discovers that the current President of France is Francois Hollande.

By choosing not to attend, Obama gave a virtual bear hug to the Radical Islamists who murdered 12 French citizens, who were merely engaging in free speech as satirical cartoonists.

Obama's inaction likewise gave his secret approval of every heinous act of terror committed by Radical Muslims past, present and future.

In my humble opinion, based on his every day behavior and his past upbringing, Obama is simultaneously a Radical Marxist and a Radical Muslim. He operates in a more clandestine manner from behind his walls of security in the west wing of The White House, or at 40,000 feet in Air Force One.

Barack Obama doesn't have an AK-47 slung over his shoulder and he doesn't callously brandish a bloody machete.

He does not commit HARD KILLS with those types of weapons like we witness on a weekly basis from leaked Muslim Jihadist propaganda videos.

But Barack Obama commits SOFT KILLS on a weekly basis using his pen and phone to further his goal of a Communist Revolution transforming America.

Mullah Obama can't use the term Radical Islamist because he IS one of them.

Comrade Obama can't denigrate Vladimir Putin, Hugo Chavez, Fidel Castro or any other Marxist Communist because he IS one of them.

Islam is not a beautiful religion of peace, as the brainwashed Left in America wants us to believe.

Islam is not a religion at all.

Islam is an ideology of brutal totalitarian control over human beings that was created by a man who was basically a murderous, cutthroat, thieving thug.

When examined closely, Marxist Communism and Islam are identical in the brutal manner in which they go about forcing their totalitarian control over human behavior and thought.

Radical Islam Jihadists are tantamount to a common bully from our junior high school days.

They rely on instilling a paralyzing fear within groups of people to be successful at whatever it is that they are trying to accomplish.

The days of Obama and his mega-liberal sycophants downplaying, spinning, and protecting the Radical Muslims with the use of political correctness must stop now.

So, how do we defeat Muslim Jihadists?

Good men and women from all over the world must stand up with courage and resolve to bravely fight, annihilate, and ultimately defeat this Muslim scourge that is threatening the world.

We must brutally kill as many of the Muslim Jihadists and their civilian population as is required to force them to stop their heinous, murderous behavior.

Dr. Randy Arrington

Total and unconditional surrender of the Muslim Jihadists is the goal.

Let Freedom Ring
God Help Us

Vive la France

Speak the Truth
Endure the Consequences

Randy Arrington, PhD

Lecture #18

Wake Up The "Sleeping Giant"

Barack Hussein Obama IS an ISLAMO-COMMUNIST.

Please don't be deceived by his slick, scripted, teleprompter performances. His words are all lies. Mr. Obama has no intention of defeating ISIS or al Qaeda or any other Muslim Organization during his lifetime or his tenure in The White House.

Fancy linguistic talk of inclusive diversity, jobs for Jihadists, midnight basketball leagues (Bill Clinton's absurd solution to black crime), and Democratic nations being more attentive to Muslim grievances are merely part of Obama's delaying, diversionary, Taqiyya tactics.

These Taqiyya tactics are purposely designed to confuse weak-minded Liberals to be politically correct with Islam, instead of scared to death as they should be. Likewise, such policies and strategies from the Obama Administration are part of an ongoing, Liberal, extortion plot against American taxpayers to redistribute our hard earned cash world wide, and to destroy our illegitimately gained economy.

In the Ivy League mindset, we must be punished for our good fortune because somebody else made that happen. We didn't earn our money of our own accord. Of course this is all a bunch of Marxist-Communist CRAP.

In fact, behind the scenes, out of view of the TV cameras, Obama is actively and aggressively facilitating a total victory for these Muslim thugs on a daily basis because his time is dwindling. Obama views himself as the 12th Imam, come into the world to conquer all of humanity for the phony moon god and that terrorist, criminal, fake prophet of Islam.

Actually, Obama is correct for refusing to call these heinous marauders Radical Islamists. They are not. They are behaving EXACTLY as the Quran teaches them to behave in their false religion that is really a diabolical, ideology of total control over human behavior. Islamic ideology is exactly like Communism in many respects. Muslims are simply brainwashed knuckleheads.

Liberals and elitist academics also like to view terrorist activity as a law enforcement dilemma and not World War III. They want to empathetically understand the undergirding reasons why they are compelled to behave as they do. I know why. The Quran teaches them this behavior.

Now let's stop this worldwide, Jihadist Caliphate by killing enough of them to force their unconditional surrender. Let enough of the Jihadists discover after death that there are not 72 virgins awaiting their triumphant arrival in Hell.

We ARE indeed at war with Islam people. This IS World War III come to fruition during our lifetimes....! The sooner you arrive at this rational realization, the sooner we can do ALL that is required to totally defeat Islam, force their unconditional surrender and subsequently save mankind from this vicious, hateful ideology.

Let Freedom Ring

God Help Us

Speak the Truth
Endure the Consequences

Randy Arrington, PhD

Lecture #19

Treason Needs Unwitting Accomplices

The most recent DHS Report documenting threats to America's longevity as a free country argues that one of the biggest perils to American freedom is the distinct possibility of home grown violence from older, Right-Wing extremist, sovereign-minded citizens who revere the U.S. Constitution. In fact, the report states that this danger is greater than the menace posed by ISIS, al Qaeda or any other Radical Muslim group.

Here is my analysis of this assertion:

A foreign entity will never defeat the United States of America. The only way America could collapse is through internal implosion brought about by heinous treason, and good men and women do nothing to stop it. As a true American Patriot, I am a threat to anybody who is actively trying to destroy, dismantle, or fundamentally change this nation. I will aggressively defend American Liberty and fight against treasonous activity until the last breath departs my body.

Marxists, masquerading as Liberals, are the people who are afraid that True American Patriots will stand up and stop their plans for a

Communist Revolution in America. They are correct to fear us because we will defeat them in the long run.

Barack Hussein Obama boldly commits High Treason and blatantly breaks the U.S. Constitution on a daily basis because he IS an ISLAMO-COMMUNIST........!

Mr. Obama literally hates the Founding Fathers' original idea of America, the concept of sovereign, inviolable, Individual Liberty, The Rule of Law, Market Capitalism and Holy Christianity with a delusional passion.

Obama was brainwashed by radical Muslims and Revolutionary-minded Marxists to believe and behave in this fashion. It's who he is at his core. He is trying to destroy the United States of America, and we are correct to be fearful of him and his sycophants.

But we should have greater fear of the morons and the so-called elitists who put a man like Barack Hussein Obama into The White House, then actively cover for and protect his heinous behavior as the American Chief Executive.

These people are American Traitors as well and they don't even realize it. Similar to the average German citizens in 1939, or Russians in 1917, these people are unwitting accomplices to the planned destruction of the greatest nation that mankind has ever know. They know not what they do.

Let Freedom Ring
God Help Us

Speak the Truth
Endure the Consequences

Randy Arrington, PhD

Lecture #20

Sociopath or Pathological Liar: What Difference at this Point Does it Make?

A Sociopath is an individual who has been medically diagnosed with Anti-Social Personality Disorder. This mental illness is a chronic condition in which the feelings and rights of other human beings are totally marginalized by the Sociopath. In some instances, this type of mental disease can be so acute that the affected person believes they are above the law, and they often show no shame for callously breaking societal rules and norms on a routine basis.

The most obvious Sociopath symptom is total disregard for the principles of right and wrong. The Sociopath possesses a warped sense of superiority, and a lack of empathy for other people. This means they are out of touch, and unable to comprehend or recognize what others are dealing with. Quite frequently, Sociopaths feel no remorse about hurting others, and often may try to manipulate people for fun or personal gain.

Sociopaths regularly use lies, deception and charm when attempting to manipulate people, and this behavior makes it quite difficult to accurately identify them. But in some cases, the Sociopath may be outwardly hostile and aggressive, especially when challenged or caught in their web of deceit.

A Pathological Liar lies instinctively and spontaneously, usually without perceiving the consequences of their action. They lie on a regular basis when no benefit is gained from it, or even if they unwittingly ensnare themselves in a cobweb of falsehoods. A Pathological Liar cannot restrain their instincts to lie and it is usually a vanquishing, personal characteristic.

A Pathological Liar will resort to spewing lies, regardless of their situational awareness, because lying behavior has become second nature and is deeply engrained into their personality. As such, a Pathological Liar lies out of habit. Lying is their normal manner when responding to questions. Speaking the truth is unwieldy and difficult, while deception feels proper and natural.

Pathological Liar is not a documented psychological disorder, but Sociopath is recognized as such by the Diagnostic and Statistical Manual of Mental Disorders published by the American Psychiatric Association.

Sociopaths and Pathological Liars engage in lying behavior for a number of reasons. Some of these motives include:

1. Admiration and Popularity

2. Control and Manipulation

3. Low Self-Esteem

4. Sympathy and Attention

5. Desire to Feel Important

6. Insecurity

Hillary Clinton is a notorious liar and in fact she may be simultaneously a Sociopath and a Pathological Liar. Let's examine three of her well-known deceptions and analyze the most likely pathological reasoning behind those lies.

1. In the aftermath of the Benghazi Consulate attack, Mrs. Clinton repeatedly lied about an obscure, independently produced, anti-Muslim video as being the cause of a spontaneous assault on the American diplomatic facility in Libya. Her obvious motivation for this lie was Control and Manipulation over the reporting of this heinous terrorist event. That phony talking point was also concocted to protect herself and Mr. Obama from ridicule and public discovery of the actual, clandestine reason that Ambassador Chris Stevens was in Libya.

2. Mrs. Clinton continually lied during press interviews about landing under sniper fire in Bosnia during her initial arrival for a planned visit to that nation as First Lady. This pathological lie is a classic example of Hillary desperately wanting Sympathy, Admiration and Popularity, based on a harrowing incident that she supposedly, bravely endured. Later, when challenged by videotape of the incident, Mrs. Clinton was forced to begrudgingly recant her fake storyline.

3. Hillary claimed she was named after Sir Edmund Hillary, the world famous rock climber, who (accompanied by Tenzing Norgay) was the first man to reach the summit of Mount Everest on May 29, 1953. This is a preposterous proposition because Hillary Rodham was born on October 26, 1947. The blatant lie was scripted in Hillary's head because she wanted to feel Important, and cover up some of her inner Insecurity.

Just last month it came to light that Mrs. Clinton committed several criminal acts when she used a personal email account and server while working in her position as Secretary of State. She ultimately decided on her own which of her emails were in the public domain and which were to be kept private. She of course subsequently erased her email server, committing yet another flagrant felony.

What Difference at this point does it make? Please allow me to inform you what difference it makes.

It is not important that Mrs. Clinton is in fact a Sociopath or a Pathological Liar. She is probably both rolled into one extremely wicked, evil woman. Most likely, she cannot be helped by any known psychiatric, pharmaceutical, or beads and rattles remedy. But more importantly to the continued longevity of the United States of America, Hillary Clinton cannot be trusted with any political power at any time because she would ultimately foment upheaval and the destruction of our nation.

My advice to the GOP: Let Mrs. Clinton talk. Allow her to have a wide berth. Give her the latitude and a generous public forum during which her own lying words will ultimately convict herself in the eyes of enough members of the electorate that she will easily be defeated in November 2016. Currently out on the campaign trail, Hillary and her vast array of public forum managers are desperately attempting to control Mrs. Clinton's urge to talk. Her handlers realize that she is the source of her own undoing and they, along with a lap-dog media are trying to protect Hillary from herself. But ultimately, I believe that the narcissistic urge to lie is so deeply rooted in Mrs. Clinton, that she will not be able to stop herself.

Here is my political advice to the Republican presidential candidates: Finish Hillary off by boldly exposing her lies. Do so with courage and conviction. Do not cower in the face of the inevitable onslaught of media excoriation.

Hey GOP Leadership, true conservative public policies will eventually save our nation. In the final analysis, true conservatism is the only way to return America to her greatness. A political campaign is tantamount to a sales pitch. Learn how to aggressively "sell" your candidate and your conservative public policies to the electorate for the definitive good of the nation. And always remember this: True conservatives cannot and must not compromise in a bi-partisan manner with members of the Communist Democrat Party because those politicians are trying to collapse America and bring about a Marxist Revolution on American soil.

Being president is almost entirely about character. Mrs. Clinton's basic character is evil, heinous, and warped. She is totally unworthy of the fiduciary trust of the American people. Therefore, we cannot ever give her any amount of political power. Hillary is indeed a world class, Champion Liar.

Let Freedom Ring
God Help Us

Speak the Truth
Endure the Consequences

Randy Arrington, PhD

Lecture #21

ANGER INCORPORATED

In 21st Century America, the Democratic Party is no longer a political apparatus that promotes freedom, order, equality, limited government power, the original Constitution, traditional American values, or Christian morals and beliefs.

Today I characterize the modern day Democrats as *Anger Incorporated*, and their ultimate goal is Marxist transformation of American society into full-blown Communism.

Combined with numerous witting and unwitting accomplices, that include race hustlers, teachers, media members, homosexual activists, radical feminists, thug union leaders, environmentalists, and Muslims, the Democratic Party is merely a component of *Cultural Marxism* and fomenting of the aforementioned Marxist Communist transformation.

Disguised under the cloak of so-called Liberalism, all of these entities are using and abusing disgruntled, marginalized groups of people in our society as the ultimate catalyst of a Communist Revolution.

They are doing this because the Proletariat working class has failed to deliver on the promise that Karl Marx theorized would initiate a worldwide upheaval, culminating in the inevitable conclusion he predicted in *The Manifesto*.

This conversion of the Democrats from political party into unwitting tool of a Communist Revolution has been building in the American political arena since 1919, and was the brainchild of The Frankfurt School, Vladimir Lenin, and the COMINTERN.

To reiterate, this is all part of the ongoing onslaught of *Cultural Marxism* and it is a brilliant, clandestine political strategy because so many of us in America have our heads buried in a pile of political sand, or are simply blinded by convenient ignorance as to what is occurring right before our own eyes.

Along the way, many of us have felt the influence of a vast array of Communist facilitators that brought us to this oblivious position in life, but we failed to recognize what was happening because of numerous distractions intentionally put up to divert our field of view.

Let us examine this thesis.

In the United States of America, if you overtly advertise public policies as Socialist, that's a losing strategy every time.

But if you label those same socialist ideas as liberal, or democratic, or progressive, or affirmative action, a majority of Americans will buy into them wholeheartedly because of their deficiency of knowledge on public policies, politics and the proper way to order and maintain a free society.

Unfortunately, our failed educational system from Kindergarten through Graduate School has effectively "dumbed down" the rational thinking abilities of our students in this regard.

Norman Thomas, Leader of the American Socialist Party, made this stunning claim during a speech in 1944:

"The American people will never knowingly adopt Socialism. But under the name of "Liberalism" they will adopt every fragment of the

Socialist program, until one day America will be a Socialist nation, without knowing how it happened."

And, I might add, without firing a single shot in a Communist Revolution.

In the final analysis, modern Liberalism is simply a word that was concocted to soften and conceal the real "Hard Kill" Marxist desires of these so-called Progressive Liberals.

Today, Liberalism is indeed the cover moniker for *Cultural Marxism* in America, and a deceptive euphemism depicting a "Soft Kill" Communist Revolution coming to maturity.

Only the weak minded, brainwashed, loser parasites will actually buy into this deceptive argument, and be willing to trade their freedom for free stuff.

Willing to give up their sacred Liberty for some temporary security.

But there are indeed millions of these types of people living in our nation today, and they emanate from all walks of life.

And, you must realize that there is an inherent danger when this political and social phenomenon comes to fruition in any democratic type of system for ordering and governing a complex society.

Remember Aristotle taught us that when a majority of the voting electorate adopts this brainwashed mentality, and realizes that it can vote itself a significant portion of the national treasury with impunity and no negative consequences for themselves in a total welfare state, the nation will soon collapse.

This calamitous breakdown occurs even quicker if you adopt an open borders policy of immigration.

The nation crumbles because the soft underbelly is literally ripped open and everybody in that society falls down through that wide-open fissure.

Aristotle argued this in his seminal work *Politics* while analyzing the various forms of government available to mankind in order to control society, outside of the State of Nature.

What does this mean for us in contemporary America?

Mr. Obama gave us a big clue when he made this statement, "We cannot continue to rely on our military in order to achieve our national security objectives. We've got to have a civilian national security force that's just as powerful, just as strong, just as well funded," to order the transformation of American society.

Today, Federal, State and Local police forces are in the business of revenue collection and in the callous denial of basic individual liberty in society, because the overwhelming, gargantuan needs of the total welfare state demand a Leviathan government.

An ever-expanding government, equipped with a huge and powerful police apparatus in order to redistribute the wealth and assets of society to everyone in an egalitarian manner is a requirement for totalitarianism.

Plus, the perpetual increase in the size and scope of government control gives rise to police powers (weapons, arrest, and seizure authority) being given to civilian entities such as the IRS, BLM, TSA, NSA, Department of Education, Medical Care.

Policing authority is given to various civilian organizations in order to further augment revenue collection and the redistribution goals of a Communist society.

This is full-blown, totalitarian Communism because the goal is to have government monitor, tame and ultimately control every human behavior, transaction and thought.

As citizens living in this type of societal arrangement, we would only be allowed to move freely inside the Zoo Cage that our "governing elites" would build for us.

There are indeed those in our society who will willingly give up their individual freedom in exchange for some temporary security, and this is an extremely dangerous and threatening dynamic.

These fools deserve neither security nor individual freedom, and the politicians along with their crony cohorts in society who push this "security drug" need to be weeded out and exposed for what they really are.

They are American Traitors who work in *Anger Incorporated*, and are instigating a Communist Revolution in this nation.

These frauds are masquerading as Liberal politicians, Republicans in name only, race relation advocates, schoolteachers, media members, homosexual activists, radical feminists, thug union leaders, environmentalists, and Muslims.

In 1911 Booker T. Washington, writing in his book *My Larger Education*, succinctly described Anger Incorporated in the black community:

"There is another class of colored people who make a business of keeping the troubles, the wrongs and the hardships of the Negro race before the public. Having learned that they are able to make a living out of their troubles, they have grown into the settled habit of advertising their wrongs - partly because they want sympathy and partly because it pays. Some of these people do not want the Negro to lose his grievances, because they do not want to lose their jobs."

This highly astute analogy on race hustlers applies to all of the aforementioned *Cultural Marxists* as well.

The Greek philosopher Plato taught us that an elected politician is analogous to a physician and that he is supposed to cure the body politic of its diseases and ailments.

Unfortunately, numerous politicians and activists today see the continued ailment of groups of people in their particular constituency as the means to their ends of attaining longevity in their position of power.

Perpetual suffering in the body politic, real or imagined, is also a primary source of the uninterrupted revenue steam that they receive.

Within *Cultural Marxism* we find such terms as victimhood, white guilt, homophobia, sexist, racist.

All of these concepts, espoused by people like Farrakhan, Sharpton, Jackson, and Obama are meant to keep marginalized groups mobilized and ripe for the eventual Communist Revolution.

The *Cultural Marxists* display nothing but hatred, condemnation and vitriol for people like Sheriff David Clarke, Clarence Thomas, Condi Rice, Ted Cruz, Marco Rubio or any other person of color who is successful based on the conservative model of adhering to traditional American Constitutionalism, strong family values, Christian morals, quality education, hard work, dedication, citizen service, Market Capitalism, and a "pull yourself up by the bootstraps" attitude.

They do so because this bucks the tradition of "victimhood" and "white guilt" and "homophobia" that they need to keep alive in the minds of their intended victims.

This simultaneously threatens their livelihood and the Marxist movement's progress, and they must dispel this notion in as many people as they can.

True American patriots must always stand up and fight for our nation.

We must not ever relent from the noble effort to save America by giving these types of subversive people "space to destroy" our beloved country.

Let Freedom Ring
God Help Us

Speak the Truth
Endure the Consequences

Randy Arrington, PhD

Lecture #22

Pity the People that *NEED* Heroes

Recently, the Department of Justice released a nine-minute video praising Eric Holder, on the occasion of his departure from public service. Our hard earned taxpayer dollars were callously used to produce this propaganda piece entitled: *Attorney General Eric Holder: The People's Lawyer.*

During the gushy tribute, no mention was made of the fact that Mr. Holder is the only Attorney General in American history to be held in Contempt of Congress, for the numerous lies and violations he wantonly committed during sworn testimony on a variety of subjects under congressional scrutiny. The video was nothing but undeserved praise for one of the worst appointed leaders of the DOJ, attempting to artificially elevate Holder's public service to heroic statesman status.

Let's get the record straight; Eric Holder headed the most corrupt, politicized, racially biased Department of Justice apparatus in history. Under his tutelage, the DOJ was plagued by heinous scandals during every month of his tenure.

The "honor video" heralds Mr. Holder as an American jurist whose record as a public servant at DOJ is tantamount to the many accomplishments that Dr. Martin Luther King, Jr. achieved for the black community. As such, the video prominently featured numerous pictures of Eric Holder standing in MLK's shadow throughout the film footage, attempting to bestow honor onto this dishonorable man. For added affect, the DNC paraded a wide array of its usual suspects, serving as mega-liberal on-screen tools, drooling incessantly over this failed Attorney General.

For me it was eerily similar to an Academy Awards Show with dozens of Hollywood elitists handing out accolades and little gold statues to their fellow, millionaire elites. Can you just imagine the divine worship displays that are currently being planned for Barack Obama when he leaves 1600 Pennsylvania Avenue?

As you have seen me state several times before, from the perspective of preserving and protecting our Constitutional Republic, Mr. Obama is without a doubt, the very worst, most failed, most embarrassing American Chief Executive ever. And worse yet, Michelle Obama will most likely be given the same hero treatment, in anticipation of her campaign for the US Senate in California in 2018, and her presidential campaign in 2020.

Simply stated, Barack Obama and Eric Holder are Communist, Muslim, Racist, Radical Ideologues, and the two most dangerous individuals to our longevity as a free nation. These types of pretentious honors tend to make me believe that a certain demographic or two in America desperately NEED to *concoct* and *fabricate* a few heroes for their community to worship. And likewise, to protect them from perceived injustices that they've been lead to believe they are currently suffering through at the hands of a monstrous villain in American society.

This *imaginary hero* dynamic is strangely similar to the "Dear Leader" treatment we have witnessed in the past, as all totalitarian regimes continuously heaped godlike praise upon their political leaders (Vladimir Lenin, Joseph Stalin, Adolf Hitler, Mao Zedong, Fidel Castro, Kim Jong-Un).

Of course, this is a fundamental tenet of the "human engineering" which occurs on a daily basis in every Communist nation or inside of a Muslim Mosque. Only the weak-minded or the frightened members of a society are caught up in this type of nonsensical hoopla.

Remember this age-old axiom: Those who do not know history are destined to repeat it, and often at their own peril. Therefore, I argue that the time is ripe for us to reach back into antiquity and study some of the great lessons that history has provided to us living today in 21st Century America.

To bestow honor upon fallen Greek soldiers, the renowned Athenian General Pericles delivered his famous Funeral Address in 430 B.C. Let's examine some of the profound wisdom contained in Pericles's speech, and determine if it is valid and useful to us in contemporary American society.

"Our government is called a Democracy because it is in the hands of the many, not the few. Our laws secure equal justice for all in their private disputes, and our public opinion welcomes and honors talent in every kind of achievement, not for any secular reason, but on grounds of excellence alone. And as we give free play to all in our public life, so we carry the same spirit into our daily relations with one another. We are not angry with our neighbor if he does what he likes, nor do we put on our sour looks at him, which though harmless, are unpleasant.

We are open and friendly in our private relations, and in our public acts we keep strictly within the law. We recognize the restraint of reverence; we are obedient to officials and laws, especially in the laws that protect the oppressed and to the unwritten laws whose violation brings admitted shame. We love beauty without extravagance, and wisdom without unmanliness. We employ wealth, not as a means to vanity and ostentation, but as an opportunity for service. To acknowledge poverty is no disgrace; the true disgrace is in making no effort to overcome it. The great impediment to action is the lack of full information, which is gained by rational discussion prior to action. True, patriotic Athenians yield to no one in independence of spirit, versatility of accomplishment, and complete self-reliance in our being."

When Pericles delivered this oration in 5th Century Greece, philosophy in its original form meant love of wisdom, love of knowledge, love of Truth. As such, philosophy in ancient Athens was not a Major or a Minor field of study at a University, but the progression of learning as individuals matured. Emphasis was focused on the human process, the search for knowledge and perception, regardless of what was ultimately revealed to be the Truth.

But Truth seeking can be an uncomfortable experience for human beings because it requires us to use the analytical part of our brain, devoid from any biasing emotion or prejudicial feeling. Therefore, the impetus for true knowledge is not only intellectual curiosity, but also a high degree of moral courage in the basic character of a Truth seeker.

During philosophical activity, trepidation often interferes with free investigation and the progress of true knowledge in society. For instance, in 21st Century America, vested social interests with their "snake oil" practitioners and so-called "victims" of unfair practices in society, often stand as an obstacle to people actually seeking and discovering the Truth.

These so-called heroes of vested social interest purposely keep their constituents in the dark with brainwashing techniques, because their continued ignorance is the ultimate source of their financial longevity and their phony heroic status. It is typically just a few groups in society that *construct* false heroes because their demographic desperately needs *champions* (like Mrs. Clinton has asked to be) to bolster a failed group of people.

We have plenty of unsung, unheralded, true American Heroes who don't need adulation, and in fact actively shy away from that type of acclaim.

Socrates at his trial made this stunning claim: *The unexamined life is not worth living.* Meaning that human beings must constantly search for the Truth and examine themselves to ensure that they are of virtuous moral character.

As I have stated previously, America will never be destroyed from the outside. If we falter and lose our freedoms, it will be because we destroyed ourselves from within.

Cicero taught us that "a nation can survive its fools and even the ambitious. But it cannot survive treason from within. An enemy at the gates is less formidable, for he is known and carries his banner openly. But the traitor moves amongst those within the gates freely, his sly whispers rustling through all the alleys, heard in the halls of government itself. For the traitor appears not a traitor; he speaks in accents familiar to his victims, and he wears their face and their arguments, he appeals to the baseness that lies deep within the hearts of men. He rots the soul of a nation, he works secretly and unknown in the night to undermine the pillars of the city, he infects the body politic so that it can no longer resist. A murderer is less to fear. The traitor is the plague."

When combined with both witting and unwitting accomplices, a traitor who is falsely hyped as the hero of a nation or the savior of a certain demographic, that individual is the most dangerous man of all. They are dangerous because they masquerade as a savior or a hero while operating under the principles of Cultural Marxism, and their nefarious intentions of cultivating a Communist Revolution in America by utilizing the grievance industry as their springboard.

Let us all learn from history because if we don't, we are doomed to repeat the same mistakes of the past.

Let Freedom Ring
God Help Us

Speak the Truth
Endure the Consequences

Randy Arrington, PhD

Lecture #23

Say it Ain't so Joe....!

Karl Marx envisioned economics as the primary vehicle that instigated social change in human history, and it did so in a predictable, dialectic manner.

In his *Communist Manifesto* Marx theorized: "the history of all hitherto existing society is the history of class struggle." He boldly predicted that workers of the world (the "proletariat") would eventually unite and rise up to start an inevitable, unstoppable, global war against the alienating oppression emanating from Capitalist economic systems. As such, Marx believed that the eventual upheaval must be an ongoing aggression, a synchronized, worldwide calamity.

Because advanced economic development took primacy over politics in his philosophy, this violent Communist Revolution would begin first in the rich, Capitalist, industrialized nations of Europe then quickly spread internationally. "A spectre is haunting Europe—the spectre of Communism" was Marx's chilling warning.

Therefore, Marxists were advised to be patient and wait for Capitalism to build up its grand economic superstructure, as it simultaneously alienated the proletariat more and more with each passing day, thereby digging its own grave during this maturation process. When economic conditions were ripe for revolution, all capitalist nations and their existing societal relationships would collapse under the weight of Capitalism, eventually resulting in a peaceful, classless, new world order, once the violence subsided.

This societal transformation to harmony and bliss would evolve during two generations of human engineering managed by socialist rulers ("social democrats"), but orchestrated by the proletariat. Ultimately, Karl Marx predicted a "Dictatorship of the Proletariat" and that the state (the governing apparatus) would incrementally disappear and finally "wither away" because there would be no need for alienation and oppression in the newly established, Communist utopia.

To date, a Communist Revolution has never occurred the way Karl Marx hypothesized. So from his perspective, Marxist sycophants still need to be patient for Capitalist economic systems to naturally ripen then decay, and fall from the societal vine.

Unfortunately, most Communist politicians, activists, and academics are not a tolerant bunch of guys and dolls. But they are adept at making excuses, engaging in demagoguery and fomenting revolution in a more surreptitious fashion.

Intolerant Progressives (think Communists) typically look for minor flaws in Marxist Theory and for ways to explain away, re-interpret, or bypass elements that Marx argued were crucial for Communism to successfully inherit the world. Re-interpretation of Marxism has been a conduit through which thousands of professors have earned tenure at various universities all over the globe.

In the empirical realm, Vladimir Lenin and the Bolsheviks brought Marxism to a forced fruition in Tsarist Russia, an extremely backward, peasant, agrarian nation; the exact opposite of what Marx had foreseen. Lenin did so out of expedience and because of an adjusted understanding of Marxism, outlined in his pamphlet *What is to be Done*.

In this piece, Lenin argued that politics was the undergirding catalyst in history that provoked social change, not solely economic conditions. He likewise postulated that the Russian peasantry was not ready for revolution and that sustaining socialism in one nation was how Communist insurrection would be initiated.

From this inauguration, Communist tentacles could then unfurl globally in an incremental fashion from the source society. Therefore, political revolutionaries must lead, nurture and coerce Communist hostility by creating a "vanguard of the people."

Lenin called this a "Dictatorship over the Proletariat" and their job was to keep the populace in a constant state of turmoil, distrust and unrest. Lenin's addition of this full-time, professional revolutionary was his most important contribution to Marist Theory.

Since Lenin adamantly believed Marxism would consume humanity and rule over all the Earth, shortly after the 1917 Russian Revolution, he immediately created a transnational organization called the Communist International. In Lenin's thinking, the COMINTERN would begin the slow process of planting seeds and actively cultivating the international community, rendering it eventually suitable for Communist revolt.

This is where and how Cultural Marxism first came into existence, and been promoted worldwide in covert fashion to disguise the true goal of individuals and groups who enthusiastically and relentlessly promulgate it. Although first created by Lenin, Cultural Marxism was refined at the Frankfurt School of Marxism in 1923, then perfected by Antonio Gramsci, Saul Alinsky, and several Columbia University Professors (think Cloward & Piven).

In contemporary America, the political term "Progressive" is nothing more than a euphemism for clandestine Communists who utilize the principles of Cultural Marxism to nurture Socialist rebellion.

Progressives engage in this nefarious, secretive behavior without having the guts to admit their true, revolutionary goals in public.

So, how long have Cultural Marxists been scattering the seeds of Communist Transformation in the United States of America, the most powerful and politically stable nation of The West? And what are their basic tactics?

First, Cultural Marxism continuously throws darts of destructive criticism at Western civilization and the undergirding values that bolster it. Convincing weak-minded people that they are innocent victims in their plight is key to the success of Cultural Marxism.

During their recruitment process, the Cultural Marxist identifies a culprit causing the predicament of the gullible, demoralized people in the masses. Then he promises that once entrusted with absolute power, he will avenge those oppressed people in society by exacting a well-deserved revenge against their nemesis.

The goal is to successfully inculcate this psychological "victim" ideology into the minds of a requisite number of individuals within the population, so they will learn to hate their birth nation and their own upbringing. This mindset renders these people ripe for Communist insurgency.

Cultural Marxism is also the birthplace of political correctness in American society today, and Progressives have used this tactic to infiltrate and corrupt the traditional family, schools, churches, government, entertainment, media, civic organizations, science, literature and to actually re-write human history.

Using the tactics of Political Correctness, everything about Western civilization must be attacked, mocked and ridiculed. All of the world's problems were to be blamed on the failings of Western culture in general and Capitalism in specific. To reiterate, through the construct of Cultural Pessimism, citizens begin to despise their own society, despite having experienced tremendous personal success in life.

For instance, Hitler's Propaganda Minister Joseph Goebbels was convinced that if a lie was repeated often enough and loud enough it becomes the truth in many people's minds. Joseph Stalin firmly believed this premise as well, and it has proven to be a highly effective tool to brainwash and control naive people. Thus, using the strategy and tactics contained in Cultural Marxism, terrified human beings could be manipulated into desiring, or actually begging for a Socialist makeover.

Instead of a disgruntled working class being the ultimate instigator of a Communist Revolution, marginalized groups would be the stimulus leading the way toward violent, socio-economic change. Alienated groups like activist homosexuals, feminists, and black militants would use Political Correctness and Cultural Terrorism to wage war against white males, Christians, heterosexuals, capitalists and all things that were founded on traditional Western values and morals. Of course the so-called victim groups would be defended and exalted, as public debate was stifled and suffocated.

Due to the perfection of the strategy and tactics contained in Cultural Marxism, there have been and currently are untold numbers of undercover Communists operating in every sector of American society. And they are still percolating the coffee grounds of an inevitable (in their minds) Communist overthrow of the USA as I write this article.

For example, in the 1950's during opening volleys of The Cold War, Senator Joe McCarthy was absolutely correct in his assertion that Communists had penetrated into our federal government. This result was due primarily to Soviet espionage but was likewise successfully partnered with both witting and unwitting American accomplices to heinous treason. In retrospect, the vilified politician from Wisconsin was merely attempting to uncover the true nature of the Communist

Party of the United States, and to root out a vast Left-Wing conspiracy of pro-Soviet agitators. In reality it was a network of Communist subversion agents, actively lobbying Congress, answering directly to Joseph Stalin.

Today, the man and the myth are not easily understood because Cultural Marxists have successfully frozen McCarthy in time and made his name tantamount to an Ebola virus infecting the body politic. Say it Ain't So Joe! But it was indeed the case. Joe McCarthy was a good man and he was correct in his allegations about Communist infiltrators.

But because of the effectiveness of Cultural Marxism, the Communist infiltration has gone much deeper and is much more widespread today in contemporary America. In 2015, we have an Islamo-Communist who occupies The White House, aggressively pushing a radical socialist agenda on a daily basis into every sector of American life. And nobody in Washington has the courage to stop Mr. Obama's assault on our Constitution or his diminishing of traditional American values. It seems as though nobody in a position of political power wants to stop the destruction of our country and our freedom.

I argue that there are a significant number of undercover Communists, Progressives, Democrats, Mega-Liberals, Islamists (they are basically the same ideologically) who are still working in a vast Left-Wing conspiracy to destroy America and transform us into a Communist society.

Congressman Joe Wilson shouted out to Americans that Barack Hussein Obama was a liar. In my humble opinion, Mr. Obama is the equivalent of Mrs. Clinton. They are both sociopaths and pathological liars who can't stop lying. And neither one can be cured by any known pharmaceutical, psychological or "beads and rattles" remedy.

Even Joe Biden warned us that Mr. Obama was not ready to be president because he is incompetent to handle any type of foreign affairs crisis. But Uncle Joe, tagging along for the roller-coaster ride of his life, wasn't intelligent enough to realize that Obama is simply a Communist Revolutionary seeking to destroy the USA.

Cultural Marxism has been a slow growing cancer for almost one hundred years. In the past half century, that cancer has rapidly metastasized into every part of the United States of America. We must use all means available to eradicate this Marxist Communist tumor once and for all to cure the body of the American nation and ensure our continued longevity as a free society.

Socialism has a record of failure so blatant, so utterly abysmal that only a so-called intellect, only an academic, only an activist, only a politician could ignore it or evade it. Then they brainwash unwitting accomplices within the general population into believing Communism would be utopia on Earth.

Here is Dr. A's advice:

Why is this important to you personally?

Barack Hussein Obama is an Islamo-Communist. He is trying to destroy America and transform our nation into a Communist dictatorship not a socialist utopia.

Wake up. Get informed. Get educated. Learn the truth before our nation is flushed down Obama's Communist toilet. Don't remain brainwashed by the Cultural Marxists. Don't remain conveniently ignorant.

It's never a good time to be ignorant, with your head buried deep in the sand like a cowardly ostrich. Ignorance is NOT Bliss. Wallowing in ignorance is stupid, and you just can't fix stupid. Don't set yourself, your family and your nation up for failure.

The "Five Joes" discussed in the article were all CORRECT in their assertions....!

Let Freedom Ring
God Help Us

Speak the Truth
Endure the Consequences

Randy Arrington, PhD

Lecture #24

The *New* Communist Man

No systematic examination of politics and societal relations can be productive unless it is based on an attempt to fully understand human nature and the behavioral motivations that compel man to act.

Although somewhat archaic in this 21ˢᵗ Century era of self-identifying social constructs and smart phone selfies, Greek philosopher Plato's unique perception of the intricacy of human nature remains quite extraordinary. This is perhaps the primary reason that the ancient Athenian theorist continues to have such a strong impact on western political thought, precisely because his explanation of politics and political behavior is grounded on a theory of man's fundamental nature.

Social relations and the political dilemmas they typically engender must never be studied or managed in segregation. At their core, political problems are human conundrums, permeated with all the rational, irrational and conflicting components intermingled in the web of human existence. Taming and domesticating man's unreasonable forces and channeling them into socially desirable demeanor, is and should be an overarching goal of political science research and analysis. As such, the manner in which a nation state could best achieve freedom, security, strength and cohesion from proper ordering of society was the undergirding question of Social Contract political philosophers.

In the field of psychoanalysis, Sigmund Freud explained man's behavior in modern civilization as emanating from two basic categories of motivation: Man's natural impulse to Love and Cooperate (the *Eros* instinct) and Man's natural impulse to Attack and Destroy (the *Death* instinct).

Modern civilization arose out of the chaotic State of Nature because man eventually learned the value of re-directing his narrow love of family into a broader allegiance for the group, the community, the society and finally the state. And yet this redirection of love by man tends to simultaneously produce the type of disappointment and hostility that reinforce the aggressive instincts of human nature. Thus the march of civilized society is a relentless battle between the collective and the hostile compulsions of mankind. Freud argues that this natural, all-encompassing conflict in social relations and the frustrations it creates, compel human beings to adopt antagonistic viewpoints toward themselves and others.

In his *Manifesto*, Karl Marx argued that abolishing private property would eliminate personal and collective aggressions because there would be no need for oppression and alienation in a Communist utopia. But in any nation where a pseudo Marxist Revolution has succeeded, a reign of Socialist tranquility has never been realized. In fact, persecution of conquered people by professional Communist Revolutionaries, further motivated these political elites to direct their onslaught against the entire world, in keeping with the Marxist blueprint.

To reiterate, Freud stipulates that cultural evolution cannot be fully controlled because of the constant struggle between the competing, instinctual forces of Love and Death, and that these psychoanalytic models are the primary instigators of human behavior. But in the minds of many Communist philosophers, if this battle between rival behavioral stimuli could be eliminated through human re-engineering, a loving, cooperative, Socialist utopia could eventually be established worldwide. This is the undergirding principle in the concept known as The *New* Communist Man and it fuels Cultural Marxism and Political Correctness today in the enlightened world.

I argue that all human behavior is motivated by need, not by primitive instincts as Freud postulates. In reality, human behavior follows Abraham Maslow's Hierarchy of Needs to the letter of his theory. Maslow's hierarchy implies that human beings are prompted to satisfy basic needs before progressing on to other, more complex requirements. Maslow was a Humanist Psychologist who firmly believed that man has an inborn desire to be self-actualized and to eventually be all that he can be (as U.S. Army commercials always say). But in order to achieve this pinnacle goal, a number of more basic needs must first be satiated; rudimentary necessities such as food, safety, love, and self-esteem.

Maslow's pyramid depiction of his thesis starts with the fundamental needs situated at the bottom of that psychological paradigm, progressing up to the top where the highest human necessity of all is located. Physiological essentials of primitive survival like air, food, water, and sleep represent the foundation of this pyramid. Next up are the Security Needs like safety, shelter, employment, and health care. Followed by the Social Needs of belonging, love and affection.

Esteem Needs like accomplishment, individual value, and social recognition are the fourth plateau in the hierarchy leading upward to the peak demands which are the Self-Actualization desires of mankind. The apex of Maslow's Pyramid is the point in human existence when people are self-aware and secure enough in their lower cravings having been met that they can now safely pursue things like personal growth and fulfilling their destiny.

Dr. A teaches that all human behavior is motivated by need. For example, I drink from a water fountain at Disneyland because I am thirsty. I take classes at a community college so that I can eventually find a good job, buy bottled water and feed myself. I hand you a bouquet of fresh flowers so that you might develop affection for me, then perhaps we can raise a family for which we will keep a roof over their heads and food on the table. I donate money to a local charity in order to be formally recognized by my community as a philanthropist. I teach at a university and write scholarly articles so that I can grow as a human being and pass on traditional values like Freedom, Patriotism and The Truth thus enabling others to reach their highest individual potential.

Unfortunately there are men and women in our nation who satisfy their needs in a more nefarious manner. For instance, I knock you out with a hammer so that I can steal your wallet and buy myself dinner. I sell illegal narcotics on the street so that I can pay my rent. I join the Bloods street gang because my single Mom abandoned me at age 13. I am a professional agitator protesting at hot spots around America because of my need to be recognized as a fighter for oppressed people. I use the "Mind Rape" tactics of Cultural Marxism to human re-engineer a *New* Communist Man and foment the eventual Socialist Revolution.

If a professional revolutionary can successfully re-program your mind and body, he can control and manipulate your behavior. This premise is at the heart of Cultural Marxism and the Political Correctness war being waged on weak-minded individuals in contemporary America.

Political Correctness as a clandestine tactic of Cultural Marxism seeks to eradicate dissent and generate homogeneity of thought, attitude and demeanor by all Americans. As such, it is indeed totalitarian at its very core, because the objective is the inevitability of Communist domination penetrating deeply into the culture and character of men and women.

Cultural Marxism attempts to absorb individuals then re-cast them as a new creature in the image of Marxist dogma. As described by Mikhail Heller this New Altruistic, Communist Man would be sacrificial to the common good in his labor activities, have a collective outlook on life, and be boundless in his desire for worldwide revolution.

Therefore, all social norms and cultural institutions of liberal democracy must be obliterated because they insulate individuals from experiencing the assault of alienation, rendering them with a false consciousness with regard to class struggle. To produce this contrived level of conscience in the *New* Communist Man, the old attitudes had to be systematically chipped away leaving people socially and culturally unprotected, utterly defenseless and thus receptive to the human re-engineering process.

Cultural Marxists could then utilize their vast arsenal of propaganda tools to complete the process of creating socialist zombies. Intimidation and extreme violence are likewise a vital component of the Mind Rape of Communist brainwashing. Islam uses the same brutal strategy and tactics to manipulate its adherents, as well as the infidels.

This newly interpreted version of Marxism views the dominant political culture of society as the primary catalyst of class struggle, not oppressive economic conditions. This innovative interpretation was adopted and honed by Cultural Marxists like Gramsci, Lukacs, and Marcuse because workers of the world did not rise up, unite and bring about the proletarian Revolution as was predicted by Karl Marx. Poor Leadership, Christianity, Liberal Democracy, Workers Rights, and False Consciousness were ultimately blamed for this failure, not the obvious flaws contained in Marxist philosophy.

Therefore, Cultural Marxists devised a cleverly reinterpreted theory of Communist Revolution, focusing their efforts on subverting culture and individual character. As such, the dominant culture of America had to be effectively abolished then supplanted with a dominant socialist culture. As the glue that holds any society together, if the dominant culture could be perverted in favor or Marxism, the economic base would naturally crumble.

Cultural Marxists actively attempt to manipulate man's thought process using constant bombardment of brainwashing "Mind Rape" tactics to control and direct behavior. If they successfully alter and corrupt what a man or woman believes their human needs to be the result would be Marxist cultural supremacy. As Herbert Marcuse argued, a new attitude of thought and behavior had to take root in America for a Communist Revolution to proceed and be successful.

Primary targets of Communist infiltration and Political Correctness in America include: Conservatism, family lineage and heredity, education, capitalism, social justice, sexual restraint, media, entertainment, political institutions, national loyalty, patriotism, police, military, poor blacks, university students, alienated groups, a-social groups.

From this cultural hegemony, a fresh consciousness, and a *New* Communist Man would be created and be ripe for a Marxist Revolution. This is the ultimate goal of Cultural Marxism and its human re-engineering tactic of Political Correctness. Everything about Western culture was to be constantly ridiculed so that eventually this new man would loathe America and the manner in which he had been raised.

Here is Dr. A's final analysis:

The very nature of Political Correctness and the Cultural Marxist message of Sensitivity, Diversity, and Tolerance are tantamount to snake oil salesmen of the old west days in America.

Don't let the Communist infiltrators Rape your Mind people.

Don't buy their re-packaged bottle of Marxist Oil.

Mr. Obama IS a "Communist" Community Organizer in the mold of Vladimir Lenin.

Mrs. Clinton IS a radical Marxist whose mind was raped by Saul Alinsky.

Dr. Randy Arrington

Bruce Jenner is NOT a woman.

Rachel Dolezal is NOT an oppressed black female.

Let Freedom Ring.
God Help Us.

Speak the Truth.
Endure the Consequences.

Randy Arrington, PhD

Lecture #25

What's the Buzz? Tell Me What's Uh Happening Inside of America

Back in 2008, I created a new Political Science course for my UCLA students. It was called: "Presidential Politics & Homeland Security" (Poli Sci 149).

On day one of class I posed seven questions to my students and, during the duration of the course, motivated them to think analytically about each using a rational thought process. These concepts were also the topics they could choose from to write their Term Paper.

I always encouraged my students to adopt any political perspective they desired as we considered and debated the different possibilities. I'm hoping these seven questions will force you to use the analytical part of your brain, and provoke you to think rationally as well:

1. Is your personal freedom a critical component of Homeland Security?

2. Who protects your individual liberty and sovereignty as an American citizen?

3. One of the major reasons the Soviet Union collapsed was the overt presence and insidious pressure of 143 different

nationalities combined within the borders of one nation. Could too much diversity cause America to collapse as a free nation?

4. Will the United States of America survive until 2025?

5. From a Homeland Security perspective, does it really matter who is our President?

6. Could the USA collapse due to an external threat?

7. Could the USA collapse due to an internal threat?

Here is the opening lecture from Poli Sci 149 at UCLA, and it was intended to be highly provocative in nature.

(Quotes from numerous authors are utilized: Robert Heinlein, H. L. Mencken, Bertrand Russell, Edmund Burke, Samuel Adams, Julius Caesar, Lee Iacocca, Benjamin Franklin, Hannah Arendt, Helene Carrere D'Encausse).

As a Political Science Professor, I've come to the conclusion that most American citizens would sooner die than think; and in fact they do so. In reality, most people cannot think, and the vast majority of the remainder will not think.

Those Americans who do think can't seem to do it very well. The tiny fraction of individuals who think regularly, accurately, creatively and without self-delusion, these are the only people who count, in the grand scheme of complex human relations.

In the most general terms, government consists in taking as much money as possible from one class of citizens and giving it to another class.

The whole aim of practical politics is to keep the populace alarmed by menacing it with an endless array of hobgoblins, most of them imaginary.

The urge to save humanity is almost always a false-face for the urge to rule humanity. Beware the leader who bangs the drum of war in order to whip the citizenry into a patriotic fervor, for patriotism is indeed a double-edged sword. It both emboldens the blood, just as it narrows the mind.

And when the drums of war have reached a fever pitch and the blood boils with hate and the mind has closed, the leader will have no need in seizing the rights of the citizenry. Rather, the citizenry, infused with fear and blinded by patriotism, will offer up all of their rights unto the leader, and gladly so. In the end, the people will lay their freedom at the leader's feet and say to him, Make us your slaves, but please feed us.

If you love wealth more than liberty, the tranquility of servitude better than the animating contest of freedom, depart from us in peace. We ask not your counsel nor your arms. Feel free to crouch down and lick the hand that feeds you. May your chains rest lightly upon you, and may posterity forget that you were our countrymen (Samuel Adams).

The government consists of a gang of men and women exactly like you and me. They have no special talents for the business of government. They have only a talent for getting elected and for holding onto their office. Their principle device to that end is to search out groups who pant and pine for something they can't get on their own, and to promise to give it to them if elected to office.

Nine times out of ten that promise is worth absolutely nothing. It doesn't pass the 30/30 Test (30 seconds/30 feet). The tenth time is made good only by looting citizen A to satisfy citizen B. In other words, government is a broker of pillage and every election is sort of an advance auction sale of stolen goods.

And, in my humble opinion, there is no room in this country for hyphenated Americanism. The one absolutely certain way of bringing the nation to total destruction, of preventing all possibility of it's continuing as a sovereign nation at all, would be to permit it to become a tangle of squabbling nationalities.

(From Lee Iacocca) Am I the only guy in this country who is fed up with what's happening today inside America? Where is our outrage? We should be screaming bloody murder. We've got a gang of clueless bozos steering our ship of state right over a waterfall.

We've got corporate gangsters stealing us blind. We can't even properly clean up after a hurricane, much less build a hybrid car.

But instead of getting mad, everyone sits around and nods their heads when the politicians say, Stay the course. Stay the course? You've got to be kidding me. This is America, not the damned Titanic. I'll give you a sound bite: Throw the bums in Congress out. ALL OF THEM........!

Now you might think I'm getting a little crazy. That I've gone off my rocker. But someone has to speak up. I hardly recognize this country anymore. The most famous business leaders in America today are not the innovators, but the guys in handcuffs, doing a "perp walk" on the evening news.

While we're fiddling around, the Middle East is burning and nobody seems to know what to do. And the press is waving pom-poms instead of asking the hard questions of politicians and candidates.

That's not the promise of the America my great grandparents and yours traveled across the ocean for. I've had enough. How about you?

I'll go a step further. You can't call yourself a patriot if you're not outraged. This is a fight I'm ready and willing to have.

The Biggest C-Word in the English language is CRISIS...! Leaders are made, not born. And, Leadership is forged during times of crisis. It's easy to sit there with your feet up on a desk, or in the Faculty Lounge, and talk theory.

Or send someone else's kids off to fight a war when you've never seen a battlefield yourself. It's another thing to lead when your world starts tumbling down.

On September 11, 2001, we needed a strong leader more than at any other time in our national history. We needed a steady hand to guide us out of the ashes. Our nation was and still remains in a Hell of a Mess.

So here's where we stand. We're immersed in a bloody war with Radical Islam, and nobody wants to accurately call it that. We're running up the biggest national debt and deficit in the history of the country.

We're losing our manufacturing edge to Asia, while our once-great companies are all moving offshore. We're getting slaughtered by health care costs. Gas prices are skyrocketing, and nobody in power has a coherent energy policy.

Our schools are the worst in the world. Our borders are like sieves. The middle class is being squeezed every which way.

These are times that cry out for leadership and we have given the reigns of the presidency and all of its political power to an Islamo-Communist because we wanted to be fair and elect someone just because of his race.

We don't have time to be fair. We need a strong, conservative, patriotic leader. But when you look around, you've got to ask: Where have all the leaders gone?

Where are the curious, creative communicators? Where are the people of character, courage, conviction, omnipotence, and common sense? I may be a sucker for alliteration, but I hope you get the point.

Name me a leader who has a better idea for Homeland Security than making us take our shoes off in airports and throw away our shampoo? We've spent billions of dollars building a huge new bureaucracy called the Department of Homeland Security, and all we have the courage to do is react to things that have already happened?

Name me one leader who emerged from the crisis of Hurricane Katrina. Congress has yet to spend a single day evaluating the response to Hurricane Katrina, or demand accountability for the decisions that were made in the crucial hours after the storm.

Everyone's hunkering down, fingers crossed, hoping it doesn't happen again. Well guess what people? Storms happen. Deal with it. Make a plan. Figure out what you're going to do the next time.

Why are we allowing people to build in flood plains anyway? If you build in a flood area, expect to be flooded and deal with it. Don't expect the Government to bail you out.

Name me an industry leader who is thinking creatively about how we can restore our competitive edge in manufacturing. All they seem to be thinking about today is getting themselves bigger salaries and bonuses.

Who would have believed that there could ever be a time when "The Big Three" referred to Japanese car companies? How did this happen, and more important, what are we going to do about it? Likely nothing!

Name me a government leader who can articulate a plan for paying down the debt, or solving the energy crisis, or properly managing the health care problem. Their silence is deafening.

These are the crisis situations that are eating away at the fiber of our great nation, and milking the middle class dry. I have news for the gang in Congress. We didn't elect you to sit on your butts, do nothing and remain silent while our Democratic Constitutional Republic is being hijacked, and our greatness is being replaced with mediocrity.

What is everybody so afraid of? That some bonehead on CNN or Fox News will call them a derogatory name? Give me a break. Why don't you guys show some spine for a change? I honestly don't think any of you have one!

Have you had Enough? Hey, I'm not trying to be the voice of gloom and doom here. I'm trying to light a fire. I'm speaking out because I have hope. I believe in America.

In my lifetime I've had the privilege of living through some of America's greatest moments. I've also experienced some of our worst crisis situations.

The 'Kennedy Assassination'

The 'Vietnam War'

The 1970s oil crisis

The struggles of recent years culminating with 9/11.

If I've learned one thing, it is this: You don't get anywhere by standing on the sidelines, waiting for somebody else to take action. Whether it's building a better car or building a better future for our children, we all have a role to play in America.

That's the challenge I'm throwing in your direction, right this very second. It's a call to 'Action' for people who, like me, believe in America. It's not too late. But it's getting pretty close.

So let's shake off the crap and go to work. Let's tell the fools in Congress we've had enough. Make a real contribution by discussing this lecture with everyone you know and care about. America's future is at stake and it is in severe jeopardy!

Here's Dr. A's Analysis:

Today, we have an Islamo-Communist sitting inside The White House and he is methodically trying to destroy America. I can't believe that the American people aren't seeing what Mr. Obama is doing to this great nation. May God have mercy on our souls.

There is no security for honest men if you don't believe that evil men will do all possible evil.

In the not too distant future, we are going to be forced by the magnitude of circumstances to develop a ruthless resolve as a country.

When that fateful day finally arrives, we will begin to treat people who want to murder our citizens and destroy our nation in the callous and cold-blooded fashion they deserve.

America's ultimate survival and longevity as a free nation, depends on developing and incorporating this style of brutal behavior, at least until the internal and external threats subside and we can return to the normalcy of our "sleeping giant" syndrome once again.

Let Freedom Ring.
God Help Us.

Speak the Truth.
Endure the Consequences.

Randy Arrington, PhD

("Where have all the Leaders Gone?" by Lee Iaccoca was used as the basic model for this lecture)

Lecture #26

The Invisible Primary

Shortly after casting his final vote on the fledgling American Constitution, as Benjamin Franklin walked away from the Philadelphia Convention Hall in 1787, a woman approached him posing this provocative question.

"What sort of government have you given us today Dr. Franklin?"

Fully understanding the inherent threat to liberty caused by political parties, special interest groups, power-hungry politicians and unrestrained growth of Federal Government, Franklin replied, "A Republic, if you can keep it."

In this regard, Jean Jacques Rousseau in his book *Discourse on Political Economy* taught us that an educated citizenry is of vital importance to the continued longevity of America as a free country.

There can be no patriotism without liberty; no liberty without virtue; no virtue without citizens. Create citizens and you will have everything you need to construct a successful nation that will enjoy freedom in perpetuity. Without citizens, you will have nothing but de-based slaves from the rulers of the state all the way down to the foundation level in society.

I argue that this schooling of our citizenry must be a proper, truthful, rational, conservative education; not the "Mind Rape" Communist brainwashing of susceptible, gullible, disgruntled citizens that happens far too often in our political culture.

Therefore, 'Strong Leadership' in the democratic model of governance, must be leadership that leaves its citizens more capable when the leader departs than when he first arrived on the scene. The peculiar irony of leadership is this: too much personal success means you have failed as a leader (*Strong Democracy* by Benjamin Barber).

A leader not only solves problems, he likewise assists others in realizing their full potential as human beings. Unfortunately, contemporary America is sorely lacking in patriotic statesmen and true mentors of the body politic.

Today, most of our politicians believe as Gene Hackman stated in his movie Runaway Jury, "trials are too important to be left up to a jury." Meaning that a jury lacks the requisite amount of wisdom to be trusted with making the correct verdict.

That is precisely why 'Rankin Fitch' was paid so handsomely to handpick the jurors in order to manipulate, rig and win the important gun control case as depicted in that screenplay. Hackman's nefarious movie character is aptly describing the exact feeling that politicians, party officials, donors, and activists have about the American public, the true reservoir of power and the ultimate jury inside our political arena.

As I have taught previously, behind those hallowed closed doors these so-called elites of each political party refer to us as the unwashed masses. As such, they literally loathe the general population because they are forced to reach out to us every couple of years for our 'ballot box verdicts' (our votes).

With that in mind, if politicians, partisan hacks, the media, lobbyists and benefactors can successfully control our behavior, without us knowing it, that is the preferred behavioral dynamic they'd choose out on the campaign trail. These self-identified elitists want people in the bedrock level to be marionettes, while they pull the strings as puppet masters.

In his seminal work *A Semi-Sovereign People*, Elmer Schattschneider theorized that democracy is a competitive political system in which the competing leaders and organizations define the alternatives of public policy in such a way that the public can participate in the decision-making process.

These alternatives of public policy are the conflicts that have made it to the final agenda from a list of potential conflicts that is quite large in all free societies. As such, control over 'agenda setting' represents the real power in any political battlefield.

In his paradigm, Dr. Schattschneider assigns a primary agenda-setting position to our two political parties. Partisan competition, both visible and invisible, is the core mechanism of democracy and it is what ultimately determines the structure of the final political agenda. If you want to know who has power inside a political arena, look for individuals and groups who have the power to set the agenda for the rest of us.

A recent example of that would be Donald Trump. In the course of one week, 'The Donald' boldly spoke the truth about the dangerous aspects of illegal immigration, successfully changing the discourse for all participants in the current presidential campaign. Trump effectively set the agenda for the entire campaign cycle, at least for the time being.

His actions mean that every candidate will be compelled to give real answers to questions he has dragged kicking and screaming to the table about hot-button issues; topics they'd rather avoid or merely give softball responses to. Of course, Trump is now being forced to endure the inevitable consequences for having the courage to speak the truth, while other agenda-setters scramble to divert public attention away from his revealing, divisive issue, campaign platform.

Remember, political power brokers, the kingmakers in America, don't really care who casts a ballot, as long as they pre-determine the choices we have to select from, thus limiting the possible outcomes beforehand.

With that in mind, we must never forget what Edmund Burke taught us. In politics, hypocrisy and deception can afford to be grandiose in the promises made, for never intending to go beyond promise, it costs nothing but the disappointment of society and false contrition of the politician.

The premise being set, let's examine the presidential selection process in greater detail, as an area of politics where elitists set the agenda for the rest of us.

In 1976, Political Scientist Arthur T. Hadley introduced us to the term 'Invisible Primary' to describe the modern era of presidential campaigning in America.

The Invisible Primary is the clandestine method by which partisan officials, candidates, elected members in government, Political Action Committees, interest groups, the media, wealthy donors, and issue activists attempt to reach a joint accord as to which candidate they should support in the Presidential Nomination process.

Behind the scenes, these various players engage in the Invisible Primary well before the beginning of the customary electoral cycle and the traditional calendar of campaign events. And they do so without any input from the electorate.

The Invisible Primary came to fruition shortly after the Democratic Party nominated Hubert Humphrey as their presidential nominee at the contentious, 1968 convention in Chicago. The Democrats did this after a few power brokers, behind closed doors, decided that Humphrey should be the party's nominee, despite him not having participated in a single presidential primary that year.

This type of secretive endeavor effectively took decision making out of the hands of the grassroots members of both parties, thus setting the agenda for the final election. Unwise and unwashed members at the bottom of the political party stratum were allowed to cast a ballot, as long as these elitists told them beforehand whom they could vote for.

Up until 1968, this was the standard practice for both political parties. But in 1972 the rules of the game were changed to make winning a majority of delegates in Presidential Primaries and Caucuses the new nominating vehicle for candidates. As such, Primaries and Caucuses flourished in each state.

This altered electoral dynamic was supposed to have stripped away the influence of those king makers in each party, bestowing power back to We the People, making the process much more democratic in its approach and style. But the new rules did not have the desired effect. They only increased the influence of all the partisan elites mentioned above, while allowing common members of the electorate to merely 'think' their Primary votes actually mattered.

Grassroots votes in the Presidential Primary mean almost nothing because the agenda is still set in advance, thus limiting the available choices of the final winning candidates.

Today, Jeb Bush has the consummate backing of the most powerful Republicans, and Mrs. Clinton has captivated the most influential Democrats. Out of view of the public, their status at the Alpha Male and Female, running at the front of the pack, has been pre-ordained by the elitists in both political parties. It will take a few huge scandals and slipups for these two candidates to lose their front-runner footing come November 2016 (a few MORE scandals to dethrone Hillary).

All the other candidates are merely competing for name recognition, their own re-election, a possible spot on the final ticket as VP nominee, or a political appointment in the new Presidential Administration. Watch as the formal campaign unfolds to see where the bulk of the money, media attention and partisan support is shelled out.

That will speak volumes about the existence of The Invisible Primary, because the decision has already been made in the back rooms of The Beltway. Decided upon in secret, by people we never hear about in the news.

Here's Dr. A's analysis:

The decision-making agenda is set for us by un-named elites on a variety of issues in this country.

It doesn't really matter who votes, as long as somebody else decides beforehand what your possible choices are.

America is actually an oligarchy that self-identifies as a Democratic, Constitutional Republic.

But most of us don't know that.

In the United States, We The People retain our sovereignty so long as we do exactly what the elites would have us do.

But never forget, having access to Truth and boldly proclaiming it is power.

As a political science professor, true conservative patriot, and Naval Aviator warrior/poet, I will always stand up with courage and fight to save America from anyone who wishes to destroy our nation.

We must ignite a virtual firestorm underneath our rear ends people.

That's exactly what we need to occur in our conservative ranks all over this great nation.

We must get aggressive and take our country back from those who would abolish it.

Never surrender. Never give up. Never stop fighting.

Let Freedom Ring.
God Help Us.

Speak the Truth.
Endure the Consequences.

Randy Arrington, PhD

Lecture #27

The "Virtual Gulag"

Aleksandr Solzhenitsyn wrote *The Gulag Archipelago* after serving as a prisoner in the brutal, forced labor camp system of the Soviet Union known as the Gulag. Vladimir Lenin first created the Gulag structure of Corrective Labor Camps to deal with political prisoners and common criminals in 1918, shortly after the Revolution in Russia when Bolshevik's successfully consolidated their totalitarian stranglehold over power in the peasant nation. Joseph Stalin perfected and magnified the heinous brutality of these camps during his tenure as General Secretary for the Central Committee of the Communist Party.

As a direct result of Stalin's notorious purges and Show Trials, the Gulag population soared and 40 million Russians were summarily executed for phony, trumped up crimes against the USSR. The atrocities of the Gulag Prisons and Solzhenitsyn's unrelenting indictment of Communist ideology literally stunned the world when the literary piece was finally published in 1973. I have often argued that the Gulag prisons were a natural result of ruthless Communist ideology combined with the dominant Russian political culture, the roots of which had been grossly authoritarian for over a thousand years.

After being expelled from his native land, Solzhenitsyn spent the last seventeen years of his life in the United States as an official guest of Stanford University. During that timeframe, he routinely praised individual liberty but likewise warned Americans about the dangers of Communist aggression, and the concomitant weakening of the moral fiber in the West, due to infiltration of Cultural Marxism and its primary weapon of Political Correctness.

The premise having been set, lets examine and analyze some aspects of political culture present in our nation today.

The Civic Culture written by Gabriel Almond and Sidney Verba was the seminal work that created the sub-discipline in political science known as Political Culture. In this book, Almond and Verba examine and analyze different societal arrangements to uncover the attitudes, values, morals and principles that combine to sustain a participatory democracy and its associated institutions. They determine that "The Civic Culture" is pluralistic and based primarily on communication and persuasion. It is a culture of consensus and diversity, a culture that permits change but moderates that change.

Significant in this type of stable, tranquil, political culture are specific attitudes toward the governing apparatus and the feelings that each individual in society holds regarding his role in the overall political system. As such, a dominant political culture is cultivated, nurtured, and sustained as the connecting link between micro and macro-politics in any society.

In their research, Almond and Verba identified three broad types of political culture: Parochial, Subject, and Participatory. Parochial Culture has no clear differentiation of specific political roles and expectations among the members of society. Political life in the Subject Culture has institutional and role demarcation but citizens are predominantly passive.

Participatory Culture features relationships between specialized institutions that encourage and include citizen opinion and activity. These endeavors are non-recursive with the governing apparatus, meaning that political activity in a Participatory Culture is interactive, with influence traversing in both directions.

A Participant is assumed to be aware of and informed about the political system in both its governmental and political aspects. A Subject tends to be oriented primarily to the output side of government. The Parochial tends to be unaware, or only dimly aware, of the political system in all its aspects.

In contemporary America we have combinations of all three of these political cultures embedded within our citizenry. What has kept the USA as a stable society for more than 230 years is that our dominant political culture is Participatory, and based on rationality, so as to maintain congruence between political culture and political structure.

But today, because of the infiltration of Cultural Marxism and the rise of radical Islamism in America, our Participatory Civic Culture is under constant attack and is in dire jeopardy of imminent collapse into chaos then tyranny. Communist Revolutionaries and Islamic Jihadists are actively destroying American's confidence in and love of our basic traditions, values, morals, undergirding principles, national political culture and Christian underpinnings.

WE ARE AT WAR on two fronts with Cultural Marxism and Islamism, and as I have argued previously, these two totalitarian ideologies are almost identical. In fact, many of our fellow citizens are already "virtual" Prisoners of War only they don't even realize it. They are already locked deep inside the "Virtual Gulag" created by the primary assault weapon of the Cultural Marxists: pervasive, stifling, runaway Political Correctness.

In the mega-liberal dominated, mainstream American media, nobody has the courage to speak up and tell the truth about this Communist Scourge or the Islamic Menace that are rapidly putting our citizens into virtual chains. And the vast majority of our politicians are Cowards, who apparently don't have the guts to stand up and fight, much less identify the Islamic and Communist Cancers that are eating away and consuming our cherished, traditional American values.

As I have stated before, in an age of massive deception, telling the truth is revolutionary behavior. So-Called Political Correctness is the Primary Attack Method of both Cultural Marxism and the Islamic "Civilization Jihad" against Western Society, Capitalism and Christianity.

Cultural Marxists and Muslim radicals must continuously smear The Truth in American society because it exposes their deception to the light of day. I am arguing that Political Correctness is tantamount to a "Virtual Gulag." It is a Re-Education Camp with "virtual" walls, prison cells, Wardens, guards, bed checks, barbed wire, solitary confinement, no parole hearings, and only capital punishment for offenders. And that capital punishment can take the form of a "Soft Kill" (stifling rational discussion and honest debate), or an actual "Hard Kill" (murder of American Citizens).

To reiterate, in a time of gross deception, telling the Truth is revolutionary behavior. Cultural Marxists and Islamic Civilization Jihadists must denounce The Truth at all times and in all venues, if their nefarious plans to destroy America is to come to fruition.

And please realize this: When those holding political power in a society allow, foment and encourage so-called protected groups to spew venomous statements that incite criminal behavior with impunity, the relative tranquility of a Civic Culture will soon unravel into revolutionary anarchy. "Give them room to destroy"

"The police acted stupidly"

"Hands up, Don't shoot"

"We must rise up and kill those who kill us. Stalk them and Kill them, our 400 year old enemy, the white folks, who give hamburgers to our children's killers" (Paraphrased from Nation of Islam Leader Louis Farrakhan's sermon given on August 5, 2015).

Here is Dr. A's final analysis on August 30, 2015:

ALL LIVES MATTER........! But as John Locke taught us, if you become the enemy of mankind and a threat to its survival, all people have the right and the obligation to remove you from society by any means necessary.

The Virtual Gulag is the prison people are placed into because of Cultural Marxism and its primary human re-engineering weapon Political Correctness. It has the ability to totally control both behavior and thought. As such, it's worse than the Tyranny of the Majority. It's a Tyranny of the Minority, as Tocqueville taught us in his book *Democracy in America*.

The euphemisms contained within Political Correctness, Cultural Marxism and Islamic Civilization Jihad, make abhorrent behavior easier to accept and easier to sell to "Mind Raped" loser-parasites. It's self-deception for dummies.

Viewed from a political perspective, there are three kinds of people in American society today. There are those people who retain individual freedom and KNOW they are FREE. There are those people who DO NOT retain individual freedom, KNOW they are slaves in the "Virtual Gulag" and as such are NOT FREE. There are those people who DO NOT retain individual freedom but they DO NOT KNOW they are slaves in the "Virtual Gulag" and are NOT FREE.

The last group of people is the most dangerous in our society, because they know not what they do. They are unwitting accomplices to the collapse of America. These Mind Raped people do not realize they are prisoners living in a "Virtual Gulag" complete with the Chains of Communist slavery and forced labor.

Today, America has been completely infiltrated by Cultural Marxists and Islamic Civilization Jihadists who actively foment worldwide Communist and Islamic Revolution. Tomorrow, you will be brutally executed or become a brainwashed peasant ruled by the Communist Party or the Muslim Mullahs, and their totalitarian ideology. UNLESS you stand up with courage and conviction to defeat this "Twin Totalitarian Plague" that threatens the longevity of our nation and the sovereignty of our individual FREEDOM...!

Trust Dr. A on this one subject: "Debbie Does Socialism" because she's been Mind Raped to not realize the difference between socialism and Democratic principles. There use to be huge differences between Socialism and the Democrat Party. But not today. In contemporary America, the Democrat Party is completely Socialist due to the infiltration of Cultural Marxism. Some Democrats know this. Most do not know this because they've been successfully Mind Raped by Cultural Marxists and Islamic Civilization Jihadists who actively provoke upheaval in a clandestine manner using political correctness as their primary attack weapon on our society and political culture.

If the Cultural Marxists and Islamic Civilization Jihadists can successfully "Mind Rape" our people to HATE America, it makes the nation ripe for Revolution.

DO NOT LET THIS HAPPEN PEOPLE.

STAND UP AND FIGHT THEM.

Let Freedom Ring.

Dr. Randy Arrington

God Help Us.

Speak the Truth.
Endure the Consequences.

Randy Arrington, PhD

Lecture #28

The 'Chicago Way'

During a recent broadcast of his radio program, Rush Limbaugh argued that ISIS is NOT Barack Hussein Obama's number one enemy. He stated that Obama's primary antagonist is the Republican Party. Well folks, you really need to trust Dr. A on this one subject: Mr. Limbaugh is WRONG....!

President Obama's principal nemesis are True, Conservative Americans who have the courage to speak the Truth then endure the inevitable consequences. These folks are the ones that Obama rudely chastises as clinging to their guns, their Bibles and the Constitution. These good men and women are Mr. Obama's most prominent adversaries because they WILL boldly fight to preserve individual freedom, time-honored Christian values, our Founding Documents, and the traditional American way of life. And they will go into battle to safeguard the nation despite contrary or sabotaging actions by any political figure or so-called group of elites.

True American Patriots are a clear and present threat because, once properly motivated, they have the capacity to force any corrupt politician to his knees, and toss him into the dustbin of history. As Sir Walter Scott said in his famous poem ('Breathes There the Man') about this type of wretched statesman:

The wretch, concentrated all in self, Living, shall forfeit fair renown, And, doubly dying, shall go down, To the vile dust, from whence he sprung, Unwept, un-honored, and unsung.

Why is speaking Truth such revolutionary behavior in a time where massive deception is standard practice for politicians and the media inside the Beltway? Because Truth eventually exposes all crimes, corruption, treason, fraud, lies and deception to public scrutiny, no matter who has perpetrated them. And as John Locke taught us, citizens are indeed the true reservoir of power in any political society.

Unfortunately in contemporary America, many Republicans are collaborating with Barack Obama and the Democratic Party due to Bribery and Blackmail. That is why both political parties are deathly afraid of putting Donald Trump or even Ted Cruz into The White House. Trump or Cruz as President means that ALL of the Traitors, on both sides of the aisle in DC, will be exposed, indicted, prosecuted, convicted and put in prison for their heinous crimes against our nation.

William J. Bennett is a former Secretary of Education in the Reagan Administration, and host of his own radio show (*Bill Bennett's Morning in America*). For over three decades, Bill Bennett has proven himself to be a highly respected voice of conservative reason on political, cultural and educational public policy in America. In one of his recent postings, Mr. Bennett suggested that presidential candidate Donald Trump would be assassinated.

Here is what he wrote: "They will kill him (Mr. Trump) before they let him be president. It could be a Republican or a Democrat that instigates the shutting up of Trump. Don't be surprised if Trump has an accident. Some people are getting very nervous: Barack Obama, Valerie Jarrett, Eric Holder, Hillary Clinton, and Jon Corzine just to name a few."

What Mr. Bennett is referring to in his blog post is the scandalous, covert alliance between government officials of both stripes, and big business tycoons, foreign and domestic. The unholy nature of this bi-partisan merger is designed to clandestinely steal money from American taxpayers at an unprecedented rate to ensure the politicians' own power and enrichment. And naturally this dishonest dynamic is covered up and concealed from those prying eyes of the public by the various mainstream media outlets. The media cover-up represents a crucial component of the overall conspiracy. All totalitarians seek first to control, manipulate and propagandize information. As Ted Cruz has stated on several occasions, the "Washington Cartel" is alive and well.

For instance, listen closely to Harry Reid, Mitch McConnell, John Boehner or Nancy Pelosi when they make public proclamations. Fully understand the historical context for their speeches. They use skillfully orchestrated words and catchphrases that appear to contradict supposed political rivals, merely to appease their constituents. But in the final analysis, the message is always the same: protect one another's power in the political wrestling match that is gloriously displayed for the global viewing audience.

In this highly unethical relationship, all of the so-called elite players procure millions (or billions) of dollars in the secret scheme. It's basically an illicit team of politicians, Wall Street capitalists and media moguls engaged in massive corruption while continuously protecting one another. C. Wright Mills documented this nefarious activity as a potentially damaging, and destabilizing aspect of our political system in his 1956 book *The Power Elite*. All of these *elitists* know each other intimately, attended the same schools, play golf at the same clubs, sit on each other's Board of Directors, dine in the same swanky restaurants and have their children inter-marry to perpetuate power.

As Bill Bennett argues, "It is a heck of a filthy relationship that makes everyone filthy rich, everyone except the American people. We get ripped off. We are the patsies." But in this current campaign for the presidential nomination, phony politicians, crony Capitalists, and media moguls appear to be running a little terrified. The daily, exaggerated response to "The Donald" from this corrupt cabal of elitists is a constant stream of trumped-up allegations and ridiculous rage that indicates they are all feeling highly threatened. Their lives, cozy positions, political power, massive fortunes and sacred honor are now in dire jeopardy of unraveling.

Mr. Trump doesn't need anybody to finance his run for the presidency. And, all propaganda aside, members of the Washington Cartel fully realize that Trump could actually win the GOP nomination. He could eventually win the Presidency and upset their "apple cart" inside the sheltered confines of the DC bubble. Donald Trump is not just the obvious subject of a humorous monologue on late night television, no matter how diligently the elites strive make it appear that way on a daily basis. It is not an accident that all of the elite players are actively conspiring to terminate the New York real estate tycoon's presidential aspirations.

To reiterate, members from both sides of the political continuum mug for the cameras and talk a big game. It's very similar to the spectacle of a rigged wrestling match in the WWE. But in the end nothing will actually change inside The Beltway. One election cycle, the Democrats get to play the good guy character in this political wrestling match. The next cycle, The Republicans assume the role of good guy. The overarching goal and outcome always remains the same: Protect their political power at all costs, using every available strategy and tactic. It's highly fixed activity, just like the 1919 World Series when the Chicago White Sox intentionally lost to the Cincinnati Reds. Say it ain't so Joe. But it is so.

The vast majority of elected politicians are tied inextricably to big-money contributors. And as Bill Bennett states in his blog, "They are all owned by lobbyists, unions, lawyers, gigantic environmental organizations, and multi-national corporations like Big Pharmaceutical companies and Big Oil conglomerates. Or they are owned lock, stock, and barrel by foreigners like George Soros owns Mr. Obama or foreign governments own Mrs. Clinton due to their donations to the Clinton Foundation." As I have taught on numerous occasions, establishment politicians are marionettes and big money benefactors are the puppeteers pulling their strings.

But Donald Trump is a true maverick. He is an atypical presidential candidate. He doesn't need anybody or anything but the support of the American electorate. Out on the campaign trail Mr. Trump can insult Barack Obama, George Soros, the media, crooked union leaders, lawyers, politicians and foreigners with relative impunity. His constituents are the mass of disgruntled American citizens who will rush to the polls to support his candidacy in November 2016, should he win the GOP nomination. This unique feature alone, means that Donald Trump is the most dangerous man to members of the DC political wrestling scam. He could bring the Washington Cartel tumbling down and expose their deception to the public.

Why do you suppose that nobody has had the courage to draft Articles of Impeachment against our current occupant in The White House, or actually attempt to prevent Mr. Obama from implementing his various un-Constitutional Executive Actions? The answer is The 'Chicago Way' of engaging in politics. Many Republicans are being bribed or blackmailed. Because of our unrestrained domestic spying program, the NSA knows everything about everybody, including our elected representatives. Many Members of Congress are closet homosexuals, are engaging in extramarital sexual relations, have illegal alien housekeepers, or are embezzling taxpayer dollars.

Obama is the man who greatly expanded and accelerated this NSA spying/surveillance program because he wanted to operate using The 'Chicago Way' inside of the political realm in Washington, DC. Dennis Hastert can quickly corroborate this claim. Numerous government bureaucracies are actively spying on every Republican political leader, because Barack Obama ordered them to do so. They watch everything and everybody; its part of the method of The 'Chicago Way' of doing business in politics.

It is not out of fear of being labeled as a Racist that the GOP fails to defund Obamacare. It is due to bribery and blackmail, and the huge lobbyist salary awaiting every politician after electoral defeat or retirement, if they don't rock the boat. It is The 'Chicago Way' that was perfected by Al Capone, and Mayor Dailey, among others. Win or lose, they always win when they play the game. They are all the Wizard of Oz, distracting you with smoke, mirrors, pretty lights and flames, imploring you to pay no attention to that man behind the curtain who is pulling the levers of wool over your myopic eyes.

Where is Mr. Smith (the honorable James Stewart character) when we need him most in DC? Where are Dorothy and her band of innocent assistants who melt The Wicked Witch of the West (Mrs. Clinton), then unmask and destroy all of the little, cowardly Wizards? Donald Trump may be Mr. Smith and Dorothy all rolled into one candidate because doesn't play by any of their phony rules. Trump breaks up this nice, comfy relationship between bought-and-paid-for politicians, big government, big media outlets, and huge corporations. All of the political Rules of Engagement are thrown out if Trump moves into The White House.

Trump's presence on the campaign trail is forcing all of the candidates to actually answer questions about sensitive areas of public policy that they'd rather avoid or give vague responses to. As Bill Bennett said, Trump is "questioning our relationship with Mexico; he's questioning why the border is wide open; he's questioning why no wall has been built across the border; he's questioning if allowing millions of illegal aliens into America is in our best interests; he's questioning why so many illegal aliens commit violent crimes, yet are nor deported; and he's questioning why our trade deals with Mexico, Russia and China are so bad."

Bill Bennett argues that citizens need answers to hard questions like:

Why is it that American workers always seem to get shafted in our economy? Why has nobody been charged with fraud for selling Obamacare by lying to the American people? Why has the IRS conspiracy been swept under the rug? Why has Mrs. Clinton not been indicted for her blatant fraud in the Benghazi terrorist attack?

All members of the Washington Cartel need to stop Donald Trump because things could quickly spiral out of control. Mr. Trump in The White House would be nightmare, not the kind of nightmare that makes Stacey Lennox experience insomnia. Trump could rouse the Sleeping Giant that is the True, Conservative American Patriot. Numerous high-ranking politicians could wind up in prison. This is precisely why Donald Trump must be stopped in his tracks. "That's why the dogs of Hell will be unleashed on Donald Trump. Yes, it will become open season on Donald Trump."

Here is Dr. A's final analysis on November 28, 2015:

The GOP Establishment, the RNC, Elected Office-Holders, Big Cash Donors, Lobbyists, Mainstream Media, Wall Street Financiers, the DNC, Conservative Traitors who have infiltrated into high-level positions within the Republican Party will not perpetrate a "Hard Kill" (an Actual Assassination) on the mortal man Donald Trump. They will however, conspire and carry out a "Soft Kill" (a Character Assassination) of the political man and Presidential Front-Runner Candidate, Donald Trump.

Keep right on clinging to your guns, your Bibles and our Constitution.

Barack Obama enjoys two simultaneous distinctions in American history. He has committed the most impeachable crimes of any president in American history, and he is simultaneously the least impeachable president in American history.

This current crop of GOP Establishment couldn't win the Presidency if it was handed to them on a silver platter made by the Benghazi Traders Company, Inc.

The "Invisible Primary" is alive and well but severely flawed.

The top Political Consultants being relied upon by the GOP Establishment to formulate election strategies are not as politically savvy as they think and are touting themselves to be, but they're getting wealthy despite this blatant truth.

The major political donors who are actually honest, are being duped into an ignorant bliss.

I can't think of a more potent recruitment tool for ISIS and all of Radical Islam and Jihad than having Barack Hussein Obama sitting in The White House, or riding his girl bike, or traipsing around a golf course wearing his shorts, or giving his idiotic, America-Bashing Teleprompter speeches.

Let Freedom Ring.
God Help Us.

Speak the Truth.
Endure the Consequences.

Randy Arrington, PhD

Lecture #29

How to Win the War Against Islam

Centrally located inside of the Middle East, Islam has established its latest deadly Caliphate, aided and abetted by the Islamo-Communist who temporarily resides at 1600 Pennsylvania Avenue in Washington, D.C.

But since its inception in the aftermath of Gadhafi's vicious ouster from power in Libya, the Muslim Brotherhood's so-called Arab Spring in Egypt, the Civil War inside Syria against the Assad Regime, and the brutal assault on America's Consulate in Benghazi, ISIS and the Islamic Caliphate have begun to metastasize like a quick moving cancer, spreading their satanic evil all over the globe.

Ultimately, their eyes are fixed upon their most difficult to achieve goal, the grand prize of conquering the United States of America in specific, and dominating the Western World in general.

"The West" or the Western World basically refers to civilized society and those nations that adopt and advocate specific anthropologic values such as:

- The principle of political liberty, including freedom of expression and freedom of thought.

133

- The use of a logical, rational thought process as the primary vehicle through which knowledge is gained, expanded and perpetuated.

- The assumption that individual human beings possess a God-given moral right to life, liberty, private property, and the pursuit of happiness.

All of these bedrock doctrines are vital to civilization and the preservation of enlightened humanity.

These aforementioned values represent the reason Islamic Jihadists attack The West so vehemently, augmented by strict Commandments contained in the Quran that dictate total annihilation of unrepentant Infidels. (What do you think about that statement class?)

Freedom is abhorrent to Muslim barbarians, and totally inconsistent with the type of totalitarian rule, in the form of Sharia Law, that they wish to forcibly establish over all mankind.

Of course, the Grand Strategy for winning the War against Islam must take into account that each Western nation has its own historical context to manage, different lawful prerequisites for waging combat operations and sending its warriors into Harm's Way, and its own unique government apparatus for public policy decision making.

That being said, how do we defeat this latest Islamic Caliphate, at least temporarily, and win an unconditional surrender to end the ruthless, barbaric assaults that are currently terrorizing the world?

Here are several tactics that must be implemented immediately to win the War against Islam.

1. Recognizing that Barack Hussein Obama is indeed a Traitor represents the first unpleasant step Americans must take toward the path of ultimate victory.

President Obama must be impeached for Treason and removed from office immediately.

He and members of his Administration have been clandestinely collaborating with our mortal enemy, financing them, equipping them with weapons, and assisting them in their war fighting efforts.

Obama has installed Muslim Brotherhood Agents into every Federal Bureaucracy.

These Muslim agents control how Islam is depicted and perceived by the American people.

They control the narrative and the Taqyyia talking points to remove all negativity from Islam, the "Religion of Peace."

Say it Ain't So Dr. A.............But it IS so.

Mr. Obama is one of them, and as such, is an enemy of the American people; He must be removed from power.

2.   America must take the lead in this War against Islam.

The American people, our wealth and resources, and our nation's pragmatic leadership have always been needed in any war fighting coalition of allies that band together to bring an end to worldwide aggression.

This will require a Commander-in-Chief who possesses the requisite amount of courage, skill, cunning, knowledge, intellect, dogged determination, humility, Godliness, and a deep love of America to take the lead and actually allow our military to defeat this heinous enemy, in conjunction with a war fighting coalition of our trusted allies.

3. Tell the American People that we are indeed at War against Islam; Make them fully understand this Truth.

Islamic Jihadists have callously attacked several Western nations, cruelly murdering our fellow countrymen and the citizens of our traditional allies.

It really doesn't matter if Western politicians skirt around the issue using fancy language, appeasing demeanor, and politically correct speech.

We are at War with Islam and those Islamic states that provide support and comfort to the Jihadists, whether these so-called leaders will acknowledge it or not.

Whether or not the political class declares War, we are at War with Islam because Islam is actively engaged in fighting a bloody War with us.

To reiterate, we must be honest with the American people and make them understand and accept this fact.

The unambiguous alternatives for America and the Western World are total victory and defeat of Islam, with unconditional surrender by the Islamic Jihadists.

OR.......

Violent death and destruction of America and her Allies, and complete submission to the slavery and domination of Islam.

Here is Dr. A's advice: We Win. They Lose.

4. Identify the Enemy (It IS Islam)

America and The West cannot prepare strategic and tactical war plans, successfully target and ultimately defeat the enemy that is so brutally attacking us at the present without identifying to the American people WHO and WHAT our enemy actually is.

To date, Mr. Obama and his Administration have gone to great lengths to be politically correct and to use secret, diversionary, guilt-trip tactics to deceive the American people into believing that we are NOT at War and that we certainly have no beef with the "peace loving" Islamic religion.

These diversionary tactics emanate straight from Cultural Marxism and Saul Alinsky's Rules for Radicals (READ RULES 4, 5, 8, 9, 10, 11, 13).

Trust Dr. A on this one subject people:

Nothing could be further from the Truth people.

America and The West ARE at War with Islam.

Obama's entire approach as President and Commander-in-Chief has been to apologize to Muslims around the globe and to shield Muslims living in America from any type of government or law enforcement scrutiny.

Publically, Obama continuously and laughably, blames traditional America, George W. Bush, Republicans, Climate Change, and True Conservative American Patriots ("CLINGERS") for causing the Radical Jihadists to engage in their heinous murderous activities.

Clandestinely, behind closed doors inside The Beltway, Mr. Obama has been secretly financing, equipping, aiding and abetting our mortal enemy.

Mr. Obama IS an American Traitor people (please refer to my first suggestion for winning this War against Islam).

We MUST name the enemy for the American People and our Western Allies, and we must be accurate in this identification.

We MUST ensure that all American politicians are onboard with this enemy identification and that they discuss it with their constituents in a sober and honest fashion at Open Forum, Town Hall Meetings in their district or state.

We MUST ensure that all of our Allied Governments and their politicians are onboard with this enemy identification and that they discuss it with their constituents in a sober and honest fashion at Open Forum, Town Hall Meetings in their district or state.

Our enemy in this War IS Islam in general, but more specifically it is the numerous Islamic regimes that are subsidizing and supporting terrorist attacks against Western targets, and every Jihadist group that have planned or executed these assaults on civilized humanity.

The enemy foreign regimes include the nations of Saudi Arabia, Iran, Libya, Iraq, Turkey, Nigeria and Syria.

The enemy Jihadi Groups include ISIS, al Qaeda, Hezbollah, the Muslim Brotherhood, Hamas and CAIR.

Some so-called scholars argue that although Islam is a philosophic and cultural enemy of The West that we are not at War with Islam because Islam is a religion.

Muslims are taught daily in the Quran and the Hadith that Islam is opposed to every principle of Western society and civilization, and calls them to murder those Infidels who refuse to submit to their phony deity Allah.

As such, argue some scholars, Islam is a body of ideas.

So what would we bomb if our enemy is merely a body of ideas?

These so-called scholars continue with an analogy:

The relationship between Islam and our current military enemy is essentially of the same kind as the relationship between Nazism and Nazi Germany; Shinto and Imperialist Japan during World War II.

Nazism is a body of ideas.

Nazi Germany was a nation-state ruled by a regime that was motivated by its leaders' support and acceptance of those ideas.

Shinto is a religion.

Imperialist Japan was a nation-state ruled by a regime that was motivated by its leaders' support and acceptance of that religion.

Likewise, Islam is a religion that various nation-states, regimes, and groups today are motivated by their leaders' support and acceptance of that religion.

Listen and learn from Dr. A people:

Islam is NOT a religion people.

Islam is a Totalitarian ideology of brutal control over all human behavior and human thought masquerading as religion.

Islam emanates directly from Satan, as such they are Satan's Emissaries and Mohammed is the Anti-Christ.

We ARE at War with Islam and its motivating commandments of continuous, bloody warfare against all Infidels.

Peaceful Muslims are irrelevant in this War, just as peaceful German citizens and peaceful Japanese citizens were irrelevant during World War II.

5. Boldly assert to the World our right as Americans to defend ourselves against any enemy, foreign or domestic engaging in Islamic Jihad, and that all of our enemies forfeit their rights entirely during this War.

Americans and Citizens of Western Nations must boldly acknowledge and announce that we have an absolute, God-Given right to life, liberty, property and the pursuit of happiness, and this includes our right to Self-Defense, and Self-Determination.

This means we and our Allies are lawfully authorized to do whatever is necessary to eliminate any and all threats posed by regimes, groups or individuals that seek to murder us or otherwise violate our natural rights.

Although Muslims have the right to believe whatever they want to believe, including the nonsense that Allah exists and is the source of truth and moral law, they do not have the right to act on their beliefs if doing so involves committing murder or other violating the natural, God-Given rights of mankind.

The idea of a right to violate the rights of other human beings is a patent contradiction in terms.

And although human rights are inalienable, they are not un-relinquishable.

A person can relinquish his rights by violating the rights of others.

Jihadi Terrorists and the entities that support them have forfeited their human rights entirely.

John Locke (Lu's Favorite, State of Nature, Political Philosopher) taught us that any person who violates the Laws of Nature has given up their natural rights and that it is the DUTY of every other human being to remove them from civilized society (Cut out the Cancer).

Thus, when we kill them in retaliation for their heinous behavior, we do not violate their rights.

We cannot violate a right that has ceased to exist.

6. Explain and make certain that the American people know exactly what Victory looks like for our nation.

America and The West cannot win this War if we do not know exactly what victory looks like and its true meaning.

If we want to win this War we must define victory and we must do so in a manner that specifies what is necessary for all of us to defeat and annihilate this Islamic scourge and return to a normal, Jihad-Free lifestyle.

Victory looks like this:

Elimination of ALL Islamic REGIMES that have in any way sponsored or supported Jihadist attacks against America and The Western nations.

Elimination of ALL known Jihadist GROUPS and individuals that have attacked, supported, or encouraged assaults against America or the Western Nations.

Only when this two-part goal is achieved can we return to a normal, Jihad-Free lifestyle.

Only then will this War against Islam be WON.

7. Utilize ALL of the weapons in our military arsenal to defeat this Islamic Jihadi enemy (Tell the CAG "SPINE RIPPER" Aircraft Carrier Story).

Which array of tactics, strategies and weaponry will best serve the purpose of defeating Islam and the regimes that support terrorist Jihadi Groups that have attacked America and The West is a matter for military experts, Admirals and Generals to decide.

All of the thinking, planning and decision-making in this regard should be guided by the principle that our respective governments and militaries have a MORAL OBLIGATION to eliminate the regimes and the Jihadists who have attacked us.

We must adopt a brutal strategy against this vile enemy that will bring an end to hostilities in a quick manner, so as to minimize combat risk to our soldiers, and lessen wartime casualties, both military and civilian losses.

America's military alone could wipe out this Islamic enemy in a matter of days, IF the civilian overlords allowed our Army, Navy, Air Force and Marines to engage the enemy in the brutal, all-out warfare that they deserve in retaliation for their Jihad, and by giving our soldiers PROPER Rules of Engagement.

Islamic Jihad and the War against Islam persists only because American politicians and the leaders of the Western nations are basically COWARDS, and have made the conscious choice NOT to end it.

And because of the Treason committed by Barack Obama and his Presidential Administration (this includes you Mrs. Clinton).

This is of course, a moral atrocity.

Permitting the enemy to remain in existence is like permitting known serial killers to freely roam the streets in our neighborhoods.

It is shear insanity, when viewed from the perspective of traditional American and Western values.

If you view this behavior from Obama's perspective, that of an Islamo-Communist who seeks to destroy America, foment Revolution and instigate a "fundamental transformation" of our nation, then it makes perfect sense.

8. Continue to engage in diplomacy with the entire Muslim world, encouraging them to establish human rights-based governments.

Although I believe that diplomacy is just a big lie and a phony deception that allows our enemy time to re-stock and re-arm, some civilized discussion between wartime enemies needs to occur.

After America totally annihilates our Islamic enemy, and all of the regimes that sponsor their brand of totalitarianism, we need to fully explain to Muslims all over the world that we will never again tolerate Jihadi Terror, no matter what their Quran and Hadith Commands them to do with Infidels.

We want to live in peace and harmony with you.

Therefore, Jihad is now and forever FORBIDDEN on Earth.

Cease Jihad or DIE.

You must repudiate all forms of rule by Islamic or Sharia Law.

You must establish governments that respect God-Given, individual rights.

You must have complete separation of Islam and the governing apparatus of the nation-state.

9. Make certain that the enemy Jihadists and any government that sponsors them, know that they are going to be held fully responsible for all the carnage that results from our combat operations against their heinous aggression.

This is a matter of the "Law of Causality."

He who initiates physical force against people is morally responsible for any and all death and destruction caused by the retaliatory force he thereby necessitates against his actions.

Islam, the Jihadists, and their sponsoring nation-states and groups are fully responsible for all retaliatory consequences.

10. Answer questions posed by the American people about this War, such as:

Won't our combat operations incite more Jihad against us?

This notion, often put forth as a rational, logical argument by Lefties and Muslim apologists, is ABSURD.

When we kill enough Jihadist Terrorists and so-called innocent peaceful Muslim CIVILLIANS, the current Islamic Caliphate will stop all warfare against America and The West (General Blackjack Pershing story form the Philippines).

11. Speak the Truth to the American People. Expose all the Lies and deceptions put forth by the Islamic Apologists in our nation. Identify Islam for what it really is.

On the Next Office Hours with Dr. A, I will fully explain What ISIS really is, what ISIS really wants, and where they get their marching orders from.

True Conservative American Patriots must not allow the Lefties and Muslim apologists to get away with apologizing for or misrepresenting this exceedingly evil so-called religion.

IF Islam is a religion, it IS a religion of continuous Warfare, world conquest, enslavement, rape, pedophilia, bloodlust and death worship.

It is a religion of unspeakable EVIL and any rational human being KNOWS THIS.

Remember, Dr. A argues that Islam emanates directly from Satan himself.

12. Articulate for the American people the difference between being Politically Correct and being Morally Correct. Fully embrace Moral Correctness.

Being in the close proximity of Dr. A is NOT a SAFE SPACE

I Speak the Truth then Endure the Inevitable Consequences.

Political Correctness, the most potent weapon used by cultural Marxists and Muslim apologists, requires that we pretend that FACTS are other than what they really are.

Decision-making is severely flawed and morally incorrect using Political Correctness as the guiding principle.

Moral Correctness requires that we call things exactly as they are.

Decision-making using Moral Correctness as the guiding principle is morally correct and is God-Given.

Here is Dr. A's final analysis:

"Damn the Political Correctness, Full Speed Ahead"

We ARE at War.

ISIS is waging War against America exactly the way the Quran commands them to.

The Greek Philosopher Pericles thought of philosophy in its original form as love of wisdom, love of knowledge, love of Truth.

As such, philosophy in ancient Athens was not a Major or a Minor field of study at Harvard, Yale, Cornell, Meredith or UCLA.

To Pericles, Philosophy was the progression of learning as individual human beings matured.

Emphasis was focused on the human process, the search for knowledge and perception, regardless of what was ultimately revealed to be the Truth.

We NEED to actively and continuously seek The TRUTH people.

But Truth seeking can be an uncomfortable experience for human beings because it requires us to use the analytical part of our brain, devoid from any biasing emotion or prejudicial feeling.

Therefore, the impetus for true knowledge is not only intellectual curiosity, but also a high degree of moral courage in the basic character of a Truth seeker.

During philosophical activity, trepidation often interferes with free investigation and the progress of true knowledge in society.

For instance, in 21st Century America, vested social interests with their "snake oil" practitioners and so-called "victims" of unfair practices in society, often stand as an obstacle to people actually seeking and discovering the Truth.

The so-called heroes of vested social interest (Islamic Apologists, Black Lives Matter, Planned Parenthood, just to name a few) purposely keep their constituents in the dark with brainwashing techniques, because their continued ignorance is the ultimate source of their financial longevity and their phony heroic status.

It is typically just a few groups in society that *construct* false heroes because their demographic desperately needs *champions* (like Mrs. Clinton has asked to be) to bolster a failed group of people.

We have plenty of unsung, unheralded, true American Heroes who don't need adulation, and in fact actively shy away from that type of acclaim.

Socrates at his trial for Treason made this stunning claim: *The unexamined life is not worth living.*

Meaning that human beings must constantly search for the Truth and examine themselves to ensure that they are of virtuous moral character.

As I have stated previously, America will never be destroyed from the outside.

If we falter and lose our freedoms, it will be because we allowed our nation to be destroyed from within.

Meaning that Good men and women did nothing to stop the heinous Treason and he collapse of America.

Cicero taught us that "a nation can survive its fools and even the ambitious. But it cannot survive treason from within. An enemy at the gates is less formidable, for he is known and carries his banner openly. But the traitor moves amongst those within the gates freely, his sly whispers rustling through all the alleys, heard in the halls of government itself.

For the traitor appears not a traitor; he speaks in accents familiar to his victims, and he wears their face and their arguments, he appeals to the baseness that lies deep within the hearts of men. He rots the soul of a nation, he works secretly and unknown in the night to undermine the pillars of the city, he infects the body politic so that it can no longer resist. A murderer is less to fear. The traitor is the plague."

When combined with both witting and unwitting accomplices to Treason, a vile Traitor who is falsely hyped as the hero of a nation or as the savior of a certain demographic, that individual is the MOST DNAGEROUS MAN OF ALL.

They are dangerous because they masquerade as a savior or as a hero while clandestinely operating under the principles of the Islamic Apologist, or the Cultural Marxist.

All the while, they have the nefarious intention of cultivating a Communist Revolution or instituting an Islamic Caliphate in America by utilizing the grievance industry as their springboard.

Let us all learn from history because if we don't, we are doomed to repeat the same mistakes of the past.

Trust Dr. A on this one subject:

Barack Hussein Obama is a human predator who preys upon weak-minded individuals.

He is a Cultural Marxist "MIND RAPER" who culls out the worst in human nature, counting on intellectual poverty, to foment both Islamic and Communist Revolution.

Don't let him get into your head.

This generation has been given a great opportunity by God.

The opportunity to defend Freedom in its hour of greatest peril.

To win the War against Islam in less than 4 weeks...........we "Go Patton on their Ass"

True American Patriots will save our beloved nation.

Let Freedom Ring
God Help Us

Speak the Truth
Endure the Consequences

Randy Arrington, PhD

(This Lecture was modeled after *Ten Steps to End Jihad Against the West* by Craig Biddle; The Objective Standard, November 29, 2015)

Lecture #30

Final Thoughts For Now

WAKE UP AMERICA, I think I got somethin' to say to you........!

I love the United States of America, and I want you to love the United States of America too.

Office Hours with Dr. A is NOT a "Safe Space" so enter at your own Risk.

You WILL BE exposed to THE TRUTH and I WILL endure the consequences.

Rest assured, Dr. A will NOT try to put his brain into your head.

I WILL, however, motivate you to THINK and to use the analytical part of your brain that very few people want to use because it requires actual effort and actual WORK.

I keep hearing this absurd statement: "That's not who we are as Americans."

Well it had better become who we are as Americans very soon, or America will cease to exist.

This current crop of GOP establishment couldn't win the presidency if it was handed to them on a silver platter made by the Benghazi Traders Company, Inc.

Truth is a Micro-Aggression to Cultural Marxists and Muslim Apologists because it exposes their lies and hypocrisies to the light of day.

In the not too distant future, we are going to be forced by the magnitude of circumstances to develop a ruthless resolve as a nation.

When that fateful day finally arrives, we will begin to treat people who want to murder our citizens, terminate our freedom, and destroy our country in the callous and coldblooded fashion they deserve.

Our nation's ultimate survival and longevity as a free society depends on developing this style of brutal behavior at least until the threat subsides and we can return to the normalcy of our sleeping giant syndrome once again.

Usually people who spout off incessantly about the need for all citizens to make sacrifices actually have the intention of ruling over you and enslaving you as they become the master of all mankind.

Machiavelli (*The Prince*) advised all politicians to be liars and cheats to protect and expand their political power.

So when a politician is kissing babies, you better beware that he will also be trying to steal his lollipop, and abscond with his rattle.

No war has ever been won by keeping your citizens in a stupor of politically correct ignorance.

No war has ever been won by fighting in a politically correct manner, using ridiculous Rules of Engagement that put our soldiers, sailors and airmen at a distinct disadvantage on the battlefield.

No war has ever been won without killing massive amounts of enemy civilians, forcing their leadership to cease combat operations and agree to an unconditional surrender.

This is America's fundamental combat strategy:

We Win; They Lose.

We use every weapon in our arsenal.

Tolerance is the last virtue of a decaying and dying society.

No other alternative is ever acceptable to the United States of America.

I can't think of a more potent recruitment tool for ISIS and Islamic Jihad than having Barack Hussein Obama sitting inside The White House, or riding his girly bike in Hawaii, or traipsing around a golf course wearing his size 29 inch waist shorts, or giving his idiotic, America-bashing, teleprompter speeches, or skipping his daily intelligence briefings at The White House, or committing treason against the United States of America by disregarding our Constitution or enabling our worst national enemies.

The security and longevity of our homeland can be equally threatened by Domestic as well as Foreign sources.

Good men and women are routinely called upon to protect and defend America from both types of threats.

Edmund Burke taught us that the only thing necessary for evil to triumph is for good men to do nothing.

Before we get into this last lecture on Mrs. Clinton today, I want to start the show off with sort of a tribute.

Most of us are familiar with the quote by Teddy Roosevelt on "The Man in the Arena"

I want to change this up just a little because I think its mega important for Americans to understand something about the struggle we face today with the threat of tyranny and national collapse.

I am making this change because I want to give honor and homage to our courageous female, conservative patriots who boldly stand up every day to fight despotism and to preserve our cherished, God-Given individual Liberty, and who defend and protect America's longevity as a free nation.

Trust Dr. A on this one subject: We need you honorable ladies now more than ever.........!

I've changed the Roosevelt quote to read.........

'The Woman in the Arena'

"It is not the critic who counts; not the woman who points out how the strong man stumbles, or where the doer of deeds could have done them better.

The credit belongs to the woman who is actually in the arena, whose face is marred by dust and sweat and blood; who strives valiantly; who errs, who comes up short again and again, because there is no effort without error and shortcoming;

But who actually strive to do the deeds; who knows great enthusiasms, the great devotions; who spends herself in a worthy cause;

Who at the best knows in the end the triumph of high achievement, and at the worst, if she fails, at least fails while daring greatly, so that her place shall never be with those cold and timid souls who neither know victory or defeat"

I DO KNOW that we've got lots of good, courageous women all over this great nation who are boldly stepping up to the plate to defend American Liberty.

I Love that.

They are true American Heroes.

Our True, Conservative, Patriotic Women Heroes are putting their personal lives on hold to defend traditional America from the Totalitarian Scourge (whatever brand name they adopt) for their heinous activities.

Patriotic Women like Stacey Lennox, Lu Esposito, Michelle Ray, Jodi & Diane, Andrea Kaye, Michelle Malkin, Sarah Palin, Ann Coulter, Jeannine Piro, and Laura Ingraham (just to name a few).

God Bless all of these courageous American women.

The nation desperately needs your voices of reason.

BRAVO ZULU LADIES ....!

I HUMBLY SALUTE YOU

Please remember class, Aristotle taught us that Political Science is the Master Science. Without Political Science you can have nothing but chaos and anarchy in society.

In *The Decline and Fall of the Athenian Republic* Alexander Fraser Tytler taught us this axiom:

"A democracy cannot exist as a permanent form of government. It can only last until the voters discover they can vote themselves largesse from the public treasury. From that moment on, the majority always votes for the candidates promising them the most benefits from the public treasury, with the result that a democracy always collapses over a loss of fiscal responsibility, always followed by a dictatorship. The average of the world's great civilizations before they decline has been 200 years. The nations have progressed in this sequence:

From bondage to spiritual faith,

From spiritual faith to great courage,

From courage to liberty,

From liberty to abundance,

From abundance to selfishness,

From selfishness to complacency,

From complacency to apathy,

From apathy to dependency,

From dependency back again to bondage."

Here is some great advice for all of my students:

If you want something out of life, grab it by the throat and wrestle it to the ground until it submits. Don't let anything or anybody prevent you from achieving your life goals, most of all YOURSELF.

As a Sociopath and Pathological Liar, Mrs. Clinton can't be cured by any known pharmaceutical, psychological or beads and rattles remedy. She should never be trusted with political power of any kind.

Liberals hate it when I speak the Truth. Their whole life depends on convincing people that the Truth is a lie and that lies are the truth.

All of their political power is based upon this fraudulent deception. Machiavelli is their Hero.

"Dr. A, Will the United States Government ever take away our privately owned guns that are guaranteed to us by the Second Amendment in the Bill of Rights? I am afraid they will one day, and then I won't be able to protect my family from the government and from evil criminals,"

Calm down people. Stop swinging at pitches in the dirt. This will never happen in the United States of America. We have way to many true, courageous, conservative American Patriots clinging to their bibles, their guns and their Constitution.

We cherish traditional American values and individual liberty and will boldly stand up to protect and defend them against all tyrants and "Mind Raped" morons. We will not tolerate this rampant government corruption much longer. We will install a new group of people into power after we establish reciprocal, fiduciary trust and remind them of their duty to We the People, and that as politicians we have only temporarily loaned them power.

Dr. A is ready, willing and able to stand up with courage and fight to preserve America.

Who will stand with me?

Speak the Truth.
Endure the Inevitable Consequences.

Let Freedom Ring.
God Help Us.

Randy Arrington, PhD

Printed in the United States
By Bookmasters